The Way Things Were

Steamer *North Haven*, the last of the Penobscot Bay steamboats, provided regular service between Rockland, North Haven, Stonington, and Swan's Island until the spring of 1942.

The Way Things Were

Deer Isle in the Steamboat Era

Stories and Essays by

Thomas P. Haviland

Edited by William A. Haviland
and Carroll M. Haskell

Polar Bear & Company
An imprint of the
Solon Center for Research and Publishing
Solon, Maine

Copyright © 2016 by William A. Haviland and Carroll M. Haskell All rights reserved. No part of this book may be reproduced in any form without permission in writing from the author or publisher, except for brief quotations for critical articles and reviews.

First edition 2016
First printing: February 2016

Polar Bear & Company™
Solon Center for Research and Publishing
PO Box 311, Solon, Maine 04979 U.S.A.
207.643.2795, www.polarbearandco.org.

Library of Congress Control Number: 2015948481
ISBN: 978-1-882190-34-8

Cover design by Ramona du Houx, photo with 2015 Belfast Bay supermoon before the eclipse, author photos. Frontispiece and photo page 6 of *J. T. Morse* courtesy Deer Isle Stonington Historical Society. Cover photo of *The Pemaquid* and all other photos by Thomas P. Haviland, except where indicated otherwise.

Manufactured on acid-free paper in more than one country.

Contents

List of Illustrations		vii
Acknowledgments		ix
Introduction		1
I	Leave by the Lower Deck, Forward	5
II	Days of the Buckboard	13
III	"He Maketh the Storm a Calm" (a backward look)	22
IV	Peanut, a Memory	29
V	No Good 'Thout a Woman	39
VI	Home for Christmas	47
VII	And What Life Is	56
VIII	'Gustus	64
IX	Cap'n Cecil and the Littlest Steamboat	73
X	Shivaree	82
XI	That Careless Woman	88
XII	Rockland's Ring-Tailed Fourth	98
XIII	And Tall Waves Flying	105
XIV	"Come Josephine"	120
XV	Devilish Micnopolous	129
XVI	Uncle Elmer and the Racin' Cow	139
XVII	Masters of Fog	147
Authors		157

Illustrations

Frontispiece: Steamer *North Haven*		ii
Tom Haviland with grandson Wallace		2
I-1	Steamer *J. T. Morse* arriving	6
I-2	Steamer *Boothbay*	7
I-3	Steamer *Pemaquid* arriving	9
I-4	Old Fred with cousin Charles' children	10
I-5	Freight House Gang and the hoist	11
II-1	Buckboard and passengers	13
II-2	Rusticators about to depart on an outing	14
II-3	A favorite place for a boy to ride	17
II-4	Four-master *Ella Pierce Thurlow*	18
II-5	Crossing Scott's Bar	19
II-6	A stop to water the horses	20
III-1	Scott family farmhouse on Pickering Island	22
III-2	Pogy House Cove on Pickering Island	25
IV-1	Fred Scott's house overlooking the Reach	31
IV-2	Sammy Knight	33
IV-3	Ad for F. P. Scott's Stage Line	35
V-1	A saltwater farm on Deer Isle	41
V-2	Deer Isle's "church on the hill"	44
VII-1	Gravestone inscription, "She done what she could"	58
VII-2	Building that housed Frank Weed's store	59
VII-3	Home of Howard Lowe	60
VII-4	Second Congregational Church in North Deer Isle	63
VIII-1	Charles White's house	65
VIII-2	Tom's cousin Charlie White and his dog Bob	67
IX-1	All that remains today of "Cap'n Cece"'s house	74
IX-2	The littlest steamboat: the *Swastika*	75
IX-3	Campbell's wharf	76
IX-4	The steam engine from the *Swastika*	78
IX-5	Sandbar and "Indian Causeway"	80
X-1	House of "Norman" and "Alida"	86

Illustrations, cont.

XI-1	Farmhouse where "Ambrose" and "Lizzie" lived	89
XI-2	The Grange hall	91
XI-3	House of "Cap'n Zeke"	93
XI-4	Lucretia Closson Staples ("Charlene") lived here	94
XI-5	Store of "Jean Baptiste" (Arthur Mussells)	96
XII-1	Steamer *J. T. Morse* headed out	98
XII-2	The Fiddler	99
XII-3	Steamer *Vinal Haven*	102
XIII-1	Tom Haviland cranking "one lunger" Mianus	106
XIII-2	Four-master *Ella Pierce Thurlow*	109
XIII-3	Farm on "Wolf Head" (Hog Island)	110
XIII-4	Pier and boat house on "Wolf Head"	112
XIII-5	An outing on "Wolf Head" and "Robert Baptiste"	114
XIII-6	An outing on "Wolf Head"	115
XV-1	The Deer Isle Ferry	130
XV-2	Winter at the ferry landing	132
XV-3	Ferry scow and tow boat	133
XV-4	The bridge tower goes up	134
XV-5	Charlie Scott in his prime	136
XV-6	And shortly before his death	137
XVI-1	"Cut bulls" once common on island farms	140
XVI-2	Ox and wagon	141
XVI-3	Some "contented cows" near causeway and fish weir	144
XVII-1	Steamer *J. T. Morse* on the rocks	148
XVII-2	The steamboat wharf at North Deer Isle	151
XVII-3	Steamer *Governor Bodwell*	152
XVII-4	Montie Haskell	154
XVII-5	Montie Haskell later in life	155
Carroll M. Haskell		157
William A. Haviland		158

Acknowledgments

The editors of this collection wish to thank the editors of *The Pennsylvania Gazette*, *Down East*, and *Yankee Magazine* for permission to publish the five stories that originally appeared in their pages. Thanks go as well to the Deer Isle-Stonington Historical Society and especially Archivist Connie Wiberg for permission to use some of their photos to supplement those taken by Tom Haviland. A huge help in this project was Anita de Laguna Haviland, who organized material and did some early word processing. The final word processing was done by Cathy Hart, whose efforts are also appreciated.

Introduction

Throughout his life, Tom Haviland had a love affair with the state of Maine in general, and Deer Isle in particular. Born in Atlantic City, New Jersey, in 1897, he and his family came to the island in 1905 to visit Charles White, a close cousin of Tom's father. Charles was employed at the Dunham's Point silver mine, and had been urging the Havilands to come stay at their North Deer Isle home. Like so many others who came to the island, they were hooked, and by 1909 they had their own cottage on the shore of the Bowcat.

In all the years from that first trip, Tom missed only one summer on the island. As he grew up, his friends were island boys, whose families farmed the land and followed the sea. Many remained friends for life. As a consequence of these associations, Tom developed a deep admiration for islanders and their ways; their sense of independence, their self-reliance, resourcefulness, trust and loyalty, not to mention their ability to find satisfaction and even amusement in a life that often was anything but easy. Ultimately, as he approached the end of his career as professor of English and head of the creative writing program at the University of Pennsylvania, he began to write a series of essays and stories based on his experiences and characters he had known. Some were published in magazines such as *Down East* and *Yankee*, but others have not been. Just before his death in 1969, he had begun to organize all these pieces into a book that he proposed to call *Moose Island Folk: Tales of the Steamboat Era*.

Almost forty years later the two of us, Tom's son and son-in-law respectively, have taken up the project anew. Although all of his tales were based on actual incidents, Tom's intent was to protect the privacy of the characters and places in them. Hence, Deer Isle became the "Moose Island" of his proposed title, and the names of individuals were changed (except in a few of the essays). Even so, the names he used were good island names. By now, however, sufficient time has passed (almost three quarters of a century) that we felt that any need for privacy was outweighed by the historical value of the material—a view of what life was like at a particular time in a particular place. To this end, we have added introductions to each of the stories and essays to provide context. Accompanying many are photos which, unless noted otherwise, were taken by Tom.

The steamboat era at Deer Isle lasted about one hundred years, from the 1840s until 1942, when the *North Haven* made her last trip from Stonington to Rockland. The stories and essays here pertain to the last four decades of that period. Through much of this time, both North Deer Isle and Stonington enjoyed regular steamboat service to Rockland. But by 1930, travel by automobile was taking its toll, and the last steamer ran from North Deer Isle in 1933. In Stonington, the *North Haven* soldiered on, running daily between Rockland and Swan's Island, even after the bridge connected Deer Isle and the mainland. Three years after the bridge was built, the Rockland and Vinalhaven Steamboat Company ceased operations, and the *North Haven* went into government service.

The town of Deer Isle in the steamboat era was a place of small family farms with a strong seafaring tradition. Although the first Anglo settlers came to farm, rather than follow the sea, their overuse of fire in working the land led to deterioration of the soil. Unable to support themselves adequately as farmers, it was natural that they should turn to seafaring as a viable alternative. As a consequence, men honed their skills as mariners, going under sail (and later, steam) to all parts of the world. Such was their reputation as mariners that in 1895 and 1899, the crews defending the America's Cup were made up of all Deer Isle men (including three of Tom's neighbors-to-be). Supporting this maritime activity was a significant amount of local shipbuilding.

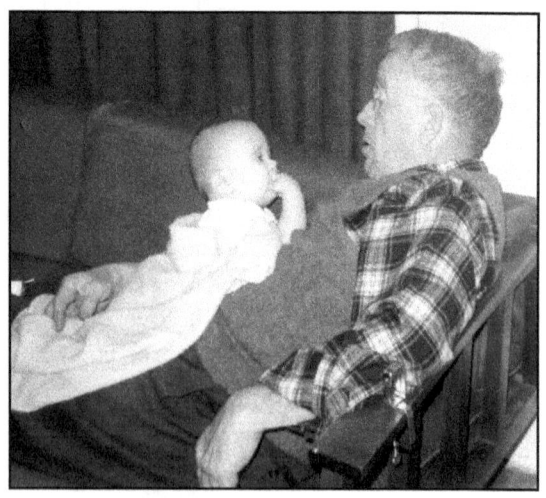

Tom Haviland with grandson Wallace.

As it turned out, maritime commerce had its ups and downs, being affected by periodic embargoes and depressions. Consequently, Deer Islanders could not afford to give up farming altogether, as this was needed to tide families over hard times. This, and the need to provide officers and crews for what often were family-owned vessels, required a larger pool of workers than could be supplied by single families alone. This resulted in the formation of large extended families, as young married couples established households on bits of the old family farms. Members of these families were in and out of each other's houses on a daily basis, and provided the labor force necessary to run the farm and man the vessels at the same time. Moreover, it was common for individuals to move back and forth between various occupations such as carpenter, merchant, blacksmith and fisherman, as well as mariner and farmer. Thus, at any given time, one might find a master mariner running a grocery or dry-goods store, as well as milking cows.

This is the world of which Tom Haviland wrote, of men and women knowledgeable about the outside world, yet independent and committed to their distinctive way of life on their own island.

I

Leave by the Lower Deck, Forward

This essay was published in *Down East* magazine in September of 1964 (vol. XI, No. 2, pp. 42–43, 47–50), with photos supplied by the magazine. These are replaced here with photos taken by Tom Haviland of the steamboats in question. A piece of nonfiction, the "Island Boys" referred to are Chauncey Hutchinson, Maynard Scott, and Elwyn Hardy. Chauncey left the island to become a locomotive engineer on the Maine Central Railroad's Mountain Division. Maynard took over the management of the ferry from his father, and after it was discontinued, was one of the toll collectors on the Deer Isle-Sedgwick Bridge. Elwyn, with an unlimited master's license, went to sea, but by the 1930s had come ashore to run a store for a few years at North Deer Isle, and for the rest of his life worked his father's farm.

Old Fred was Fred P. Scott, the central character in "Peanut, a Memory." The "lame ferryman" Sammy Knight, also figures in that story, and in "Devilish Micnopolous."

In this, the next, and several other stories in this collection, mention is often made in passing of "make-and-break" and/or "Mianus" gasoline engines. Mianus was one maker of such engines, which had one (one-lungers) or two cylinders, and were hand cranked to start (see photo XII-1). Instead of a spark plug, they had an igniter bolted onto the cylinder. Inside, two points coming together provided the spark for ignition. This was activated by a rod running off an eccentric bearing on the crankshaft, between the engine and the big heavy flywheel. This drove the rod up against another on the igniter, compressing the spring and activating the points. The spring separated the points as the rod went down before its next upward thrust.

☙ Leave by the Lower Deck, Forward ❧

Fig. I-1. This photo shows the *J. T. Morse* arriving, "with her pounding paddlewheels and her needle bow." The mainland shows in the background.

If Sam Clemens found fascination in the gusty riverfront of Hannibal, Missouri, with its great stern-wheelers and side-wheelers, we island boys—Chauncey and Maynard and Elwyn and I—were drawn by a similar magnetism to the North Deer Isle wharf at boat time, and hardly a landing did we miss. If we had tarried unduly in somebody's blueberry field, the long full-throated blast announcing that the morning steamer was halfway from the red spar, and then the rattle of the chain in the windlass as the slip was lowered to meet her, would set us on the run.

Perhaps the officers of the Eastern Steamship Lines and of the seagoing division of the Maine Central Railroad were not the equal of Mark Twain's river dandies, but in our teenage eyes these Penobscot counterparts were truly great figures against the sky. The landing made, they descended from the pilothouse, resplendent in gold buttons and gold-braided caps bearing the magic words "Captain" and "Pilot." Like benevolent despots, they lounged idly by the rail of the hurricane deck, tossing remarks to honored familiars on the dock, while young hearts skipped a beat. Those long forgotten white steamers, whose destinies they ruled—the *J. T. Morse*, the *Pemaquid*, the *Boothbay*—were gallant craft, and if they were perhaps a shade smaller than the *Lusitania*, we were not particularly aware of it.

The great broad-beamed *J. T. Morse*, with her pounding paddlewheels and her needle bow, was a beautiful sight as she eased toward the wharf, the quartermaster standing alert on the main deck forward, coil in hand. And then the line thrown, the sharp staccato of bells as she was maneuvered, the gentle grinding against the piling while the agent hauled in the heavy hawsers bow and stern, led them through a chock and looped them over a piling. Several hands managed the hawser below, and the gangplank was run out, all under the practiced eye of our fellow townsman, Mr. Hosmer. He stood at the starboard gangway, shouting, "Easy boys, slack her off a mite more. Check her!" while two roustabouts negotiated the broadjump to the runway to the pier, lines in hand. Then the jingle, "Stop engines!"

The mail was trucked up the steep slip first, followed by the purser with his important papers—a casual, friendly man, leisurely, but quick in

Fig. I-2. The steamer *Boothbay* supplanted the *J. T. Morse*. Here it is at North Deer Isle Landing.

his banter with those who leaned on the rails that lined the runway. Passengers were directed: "Leave by the lower deck, forward."

In the summer months there was a bustle, I tell you. High, three-seated buckboards, each drawn by a fine pair of horses, bright wagons, grocery carts and low-slung jiggers were tethered to the rails, often the length of the wharf. As the two-wheeled hand trucks were moved clanking in steady procession from the *Morse*'s lower deck and in and out of the long freight house, families received back their errant ones. The town liverymen—little Tom Gray and dapper Frank Greenlaw—maneuvered for their share of the "drummers" [salesmen] and the summer folk, while Old Fred, the butt of all our jokes, with his shabby fringed two-seater, would get their leavings.

Then the cessation of clatter, the whistling of new steam, the tolling of the big bell up by the ship's walking-beam to signify that all who were going aboard should really hurry—for this great craft had business to do, miles to go, and would wait for no one. Captain Winterbotham, nonchalant by his auxiliary bell-pull, at the rail, waited only for the gangplank to be run in and the lines cast off. "All aboard that's going aboard!" he cried. And we boys echoed, "All aboard that's going aboard, and if you can't get a board, get a shingle." One more island day, we felt, had begun with proper ceremony.

Her return trip west might or might not find us present, depending on the concerns of a boy's busy day, but the wharf often held us. There was good fishing for cunners, flounders and harbor Pollock, adventure in clambering about the barnacle-encrusted cribs at low water, or an occasional trip to Sargentville or Eggemoggin with the lame ferryman, who kept his little double-ended craft at the float. If Chauncey or I stood particularly high in his favor at the moment, we might even be permitted to roll over the flywheel of the old one-lung *Mianus*.

But even if we missed the return trip of the *Morse* in the afternoon, nothing ever was allowed to interfere with our gathering to await the *Pemaquid*'s arrival at eight in the evening. This sleek, steel beauty held a particular spot in island hearts, partly because her construction permitted her to buck the ice and bring needed supplies after the Eastern's boat had to discontinue service for the winter, and partly because her home port was Sargentville. On Sundays we could row a peapod across the Reach, board her, explore the shining engine room and fraternize with the crew. The *Pemaquid* didn't set out to be a fashion plate like the *J. T. Morse* with its steward and colored waiters in the grand saloon, but she was folksy and sound. On the rare occasions when we made the jaunt from Rockland on the *Pemaquid*, the steward fed us a halibut dinner in the crew's little dining saloon, on a red-checkered cloth, all for fifty cents.

The *Pemaquid*'s evening visit closed the day on just the proper note for our elders as well, for they could leave the gardens, the cattle and the haying that filled their daytime hours. Captain Rowland, in his eighties and long retired from the quarter-deck, stoutly trudged the mile from home and back with the aid of his cane. And poor Reuben plodded heavily from around the Reach Road, an ox of a man for strength but a mite weak in the head, finding simple joy when we had him stand on the baggage room scales and read his weight at three hundred and fifty pounds. It was enough to set him off to such prodigious feats as hefting a full barrel of flour or driving his fist through the heavy panel of a door. Captain Charles and his bow-legged partner in the hip-boots who worked the big weir over by Carney Island together, could be counted on, too. Beaux and belles were there, of course, and some exciting but not too wicked things went on in the dark shadows of the building. As boys, we weren't too much interested at the time.

Folks talked crops and politics and whether the tinker mackerel were running or cod were being caught out by Kimball's Head, as

Fig. I-3. The *Pemaquid* arriving at the North Deer Isle landing. The tall female passenger with the hat may be Mrs. Arthur Haviland. There would be several buckboards and other horse-drawn conveyances available to carry her and her luggage to The Beeches, their summer cottage.

they watched the progress of the boat's myriad lighted windows from Brooklin to Sedgwick. Then we saw port and starboard lights head on, and the *Pemaquid* became a slim silhouette against the heavier blackness of the mainland. On still nights we could catch the thud of her propeller well before the narrow beam of her searchlight picked out the wharf and bathed us for a moment in silver. Thick nights made little difference in the evening ritual unless it was already dungeon fog before the *Pemaquid* made Stonington. Even in foul weather we counted on her to make the difficult run through Deer Island Thorofare and the maze of ledges and islands at the foot of the Reach. Then, while heavy drops pattered from the roof of

Fig. I-4. Shown here is Old Fred with his cousin Charles' children: Maynard, Bessie and Doris.

the little square waiting room behind us, we took turns at cranking the fog horn at the corner of the wharf, waiting for the pilot to pull his cord in response. Because the *Pemaquid* was railroad property, she answered with a shrill locomotive whistle, eerily echoing and re-echoing from the woods along the shore.

On such nights none of the jaunty teams from the village came to greet her, only Old Fred from up on the hill hoping for even a spare half-dollar, and more often disappointed than not. Fred, who never took a bath, was always reaching out for friendship and understanding which was ever denied him. "Keish, you know what? I'm going to get me one of them high silk hats and some yellow gloves and have the rig upholstered—then maybe business will be better b'um'bye." And perhaps even while he talked, some hellion was loosening a nut on his off hind wheel.

I suppose we boys reached the height of our enjoyment when we tested our strength dragging hand trucks loaded with bags of grain up the steep incline from the steamer to the freight house. Since North Deer Isle was the next to last stop, crew members by then were tired from bucking heavy loads, and were only too willing to let us boys lend a hand. If the tide was high, we pushed our loaded trucks before us, but if the slip had been lowered twelve feet to dead low water, we tugged them doggedly up behind us, muscles pulled taut, putting our backs and the calves of our legs into it, conscious of admiring female eyes. In other ways, low tide was even more rewarding. Having deposited our load in the wharf building, we could then imitate the crew's method of returning the empty truck to the steamer. We put one foot on the axle, and dragging the other as a brake and guide, slid with flashing speed down the smooth slip and across the gangplank. It took a sudden turn to the right to avoid being shot clean out of the opposite gangway. For a brief period each night, trucking grain, we boys became a part of the *Pemaquid*'s crew. What men they were, with their tattooed arms and their sweaters bearing the names of other steamboats on which they had served—the *Samoset, Sapphe, Sieur de Monts*!

Today the steamboats no longer serve Deer Isle. The two sprawling livery stables in the village are long since gone; there are no more horses and oxen and cows to demand the feed that was a considerable part of our boats' lading—indeed, hardly even a chicken anymore. The freight

Fig. I-5. Shown here is the Freight House Gang sometime before 1928. Also the hoist for the adjustable slip ramp; Caterpillar Hill is in the background on the mainland.

moves in on trucks; the drummers are few and the rambling old Lynmore, their stopover through the generations, has burned. Tourists now drive their cars across the bridge ("rusticators" having gone out of fashion), and none shall know the delight, threading Fox Island Thorofare or coasting along in the shadow of the Camden Hills toward Tillson's Wharf at dusk, of the afterdeck, with its peculiar bouquet compounded of ozone, soft coal smoke, and the fragrance of the crew's mess. The propeller churns smoothly, the rudder chain slatting in the wake, the railing and fixtures vibrating gently in tune, while the gulls wheel and cry shrilly overhead, vying for the scraps tossed out of the galley. There are no more passenger ships on River or Bay, save the new State Ferries. The *J. T. Morse* has gone to her grave after serving as an excursion boat on New York's East River. The *Boothbay*, which supplanted her on the run through the Reach, became the ferry to the Statue of Liberty in New York Harbor and was then sold south to Wilmington, Delaware. Our darling, the *Pemaquid*, too, has met her end. But neither Cauncey, Elwyn nor I likes to think too much about it.

II

Days of the Buckboard

Fig. II-1. Buckboard and passengers, ready for a day's "outing."

Another piece of nonfiction, this was never published. The "captain" would have been Charles Scott, one of Tom's childhood "heroes" (see "Devilish Micnopolous.") Besides running the ferry, Charles Scott was quartermaster on the all-Deer Isle crew on the America's Cup defender *Columbia* in 1899. Photos are by Thomas P. Haviland. "Pinkeytown," mentioned later in this piece, was a local nickname for Little Deer Isle, and the Indian causeway to Sunshine was an ancient Indian fish trap.

ca Days of the Buckboard ca

Fig. II-2. Rusticators about to depart on an outing. Beside the driver is Tom Haviland's mother, behind her Minnie and Charles White. The other three passengers are unknown; the house is the White's.

You may talk about the age of the machine, the 455 cubic inch rocket V8 and the supersonic jet, but the two most exciting rides I have had in my long misspent life were behind elegant horseflesh.

The first of these was on a pitch-black night, returning from a pre-election caucus in the town house. The captain had asked if I'd like to go, and, though I knew I couldn't share his enthusiasm for the oratory that always filled the evening, I was never one to turn down his company. The occasion's real interest lay, it turned out, in the return trip home. Near the Red Schoolhouse, the road serpentined for several miles through spruce, birch, and thick clumps of alders like a black curtain which pressed in from both margins to brush the sides of our open buggy. We traveled without lamps so that, except for the lateness of the hour, we might easily have swung round a sudden curve and crashed into an oncoming vehicle—the only passing was by a slow pull out into the alders, grinding them under the near front wheel. It was impossible to guide our horse by the reins; no human eyes could pierce the impenetrable darkness.

And so the big black gelding, eager for the barn at the end of his working day, left to himself and freed of all driver control, pounded along the unseen road, an occasional stone flying from his hooves, gravel crunching under the iron tires of the buggy, the cool night air whistling through my hair. All we could see, through a narrow slit between the tree tops, were the distant stars overhead. Our rating was only one horse power, but our speed was exciting, exhilarating—and a bit frightening, too. There was always the prospect of that other unlighted buggy that might be approaching, the only late warning the staccato of hooves above the steady pounding of our own.

The other occasion was of much shorter duration, in broad daylight, and between vehicles not exactly designed for speed. But the road, barely wide enough for the two buckboards abreast, led sharply downhill to where it narrowed to cross the mill dam. Each carried its full quota of eight, the weight pressing relentlessly after the horses' flying hocks. "Pink Gray" and one of Frank Greenlaw's drivers urged them on—hands high, reins wide, leaning slightly forward over the dash, giving the horses their heads. The four beasts were able, and caught the spirit of the occasion. And so we rattled down to the breast of the dam—if at nothing like the pace of the captain's big black, still with the exhilaration of a race—Pink shouting, "Don't crowd me, don't crowd me!" and our rival doing just that. At the very last moment when a crash seemed imminent, Pink having to decide between the ditch and defeat, hauled back strongly on his reins, shoved hard with his foot against the lever which brought two heavy wooden blocks down on the rims of the two hind wheels, and the other ungainly craft crossed ahead of us with undiminished speed, then slowed on the hill on the far side that led into the main street of the village. As a boy I considered our adversary quite unsporting and delivered some heavy sarcasm at the heads of the passengers in the victorious team—much to my mother's embarrassment, for one of them was Harriet Haskell, wife of the town barber and kept the candy store.

As I have said, and some of my older readers will recall, the buckboard was not built for speed, but for a leisurely cruising of the unimproved roads. Pulled by two horses, it consisted of a long, flexible platform perched high on the axles that joined two pairs of oversized iron-bound wheels, slim and rather spidery but so large in circumference that one climbed up to his perch by way of a narrow running-board, itself a good high step from the ground. The seats were detachable, and the rear one was not infrequently removed on the occasion of meeting the morning boat, to provide room for suitcases and trunks. Loafers at the steamboat landing could always count on one of these nicely tufted gray seats, backed up against the freight house until the driver's return, as a comfortable place to relax. The front seat, accommodating the driver and one other, was raised slightly above the other two and protected from flying stones and such by a dash board surrounded by a nickel bar curved up at either end, over which one could rest the reins at a leisurely job. The two seats astern of this were wide enough to hold easily three solid built folk in each.

It was a favorite rig for passenger service; never the *J. T. Morse* arrived but two or three of these ungainly affairs were tethered among the surreys, buggies and bright-wagons along the rails of the Maine Central Wharf, together with a low-slung jigger for the heavy freight that was trucked out of her hold. Newcomers to the island, just after the turn of the century, we first met Tom Gray and his buckboard under such circumstances. The letter announcing the date of our arrival snuggled safely in one of the sacks just trucked up the gangplank, but "Ayeh," Tom knew where Charley White lived.

Tom and his chief competitor, dapper Frank Greenlaw, who eventually took the yellow kid gloves he habitually wore off, to the greater promise of Saratoga Spa, had adjacent stables in Northwest Harbor—big, musty, rich-smelling and cavernous, housing about fifteen horses apiece for the drummers and the carriage trade. For a boy these dusky caverns were a source of endless fascination—the sights, sounds, the gentle stirring of the horses tied in their stalls, the munching of grain, running streams lifted by a wheezing and battered old ram in the brook below for watering the animals or washing down varnished and yellow-spoked wheels. The drivers, who doubled as stable men, also had much to add to a growing boy's knowledge of the realities of life.

Of course, the prime reason for the buckboard's being was the "rusticator," who would get together a party and charter one of these oversized craft. The ladies dressed for the occasion in voluminous skirts and wide-brimmed hats; the males of the genus *Rusticator* spruced up somewhat also, with tie and clean khaki pants for the momentous occasion. This automotive generation will find it difficult to conceive the calm delight in jogging behind a perfect pair over the winding roads, at leisure contemplating the trees, the birds and the wild flowers or the white clapboard houses with their capacious barns.

For an active boy there were two particular pleasures: To sit beside the driver in the raised forward seat, perhaps even finding opportunity to handle the reins while the pair of horses sedately trotted along a

Fig. II-3. A favorite place for a boy to ride.

straightaway or walked to rest or regain their wind on the narrow dirt roads, staring meanwhile over the sleek and shiny backs, reaching out on occasion from his advanced post to slap a horsefly on a fat rump, or catching the fragrance when the animals broke wind. There were times when a horse with a more serious purpose stopped stock still, on which occasion the ladies of my mother's Victorian tradition became too elaborately oblivious of what was going on.

Or a lad would at some point, such as a slow ascent of a hill, hop down by way of the running board to the road, perching himself now on the overhang of the deck at the rear, legs dangling, back comfortable against the rear seat. Here he could be off and on again a dozen times, snapping photographs with his Brownie box camera, collecting pine cones, sharing juicy blackberries or choke cherries with those aboard, chasing madly after when a playful driver whipped up his team on a level or a slight down grade. At the whim of the passengers, the driver could always pull up with a "Whoa, set back" to provide an even more leisurely panorama of the blue sparkling waters of some cove, or sight of a beautiful white sloop close-hauled. There was no hurry; usually a whole afternoon was at their disposal. People had mastered the fine art of relaxing.

There were various established trips on our island, adjusted to the time available and the horses' energy, without several of which no sum-

Fig. II-4. The four-master *Ella Pierce Thurlow* riding at anchor.

mer was complete. There was the old silver mine at Dunham's Point, a pleasant rocky promontory bearing on its back a couple of moldering old tarpapered buildings; against its cliffs vessels were once heeled in for loading the precious cargo in crocus bags, piles of which still lay rotting in the weather, so a boy could fill his pockets with chunks of the crushed rock glittering with pyrites and take them home to pass off among his friends as real gold.

There was a ride out the sparsely settled Reach Road, thickly studded with great pine trees, which grew nowhere else on the island. After several miles, the buckboard turned right down the Torrey's Pond Road, piercing the heavily wooded center of the island, remote from all human habitation. How eagerly we boys anticipated the nest atop a great spruce tree on the far shore of the pond where two big old bald-headed eagles perched. Of an afternoon one might choose the village of Sunset as one's destination, debouching, homeward bound, by way of the lovely sandy crescent of Sylvester's Cove. This ride had the added attraction of a pause in its leisurely course at Harkie Pickering's. There one walked through an outer, unused store, its shelves yawning empty but for a carton or two of cones, to group around the long table always with immaculate white linen cloth, the back window offering a view of the outer harbor, with the four-master *Ella Pierce Thurlow* riding at anchor. For ten cents, Harkie provided a big pyramidal scoop of rich homemade vanilla, yellow with eggs, chocolate or grapenut ice cream (frozen custard, some called it) long before the degenerate fluff from the westward made its way into New England.

Or one dedicated an afternoon to crossing Scott's Bar to "Pinkeytown," (Little Deer Isle) in those days a pretty primitive settlement, where at the appearance of a buckboard load of strangers, the small children would pop like rabbits into the dense cedar copses by the roadside. Our father always carried a pocketful of bright pennies on this jaunt, tossing them into the road behind to lure the shy ones out. And so, on out to the lighthouse and the small log-cribbed Eastern Steamship wharf at Eggemoggin, with its gingerbready summer cottages. This latter trip had to be timed just right, for the tide served for the crossing only about four hours, at the end of which, passage was cut off for another tidal cycle. Often, wandering the beach of our island, I had come upon the butcher wagon, where the road to Pinkeytown ended in the bay, waiting for passage, Willis asleep in the driver's seat, his gray mare also asleep leaning against the last telephone pole before the cable and the road went under water. The driver had also to be sure of his tides when he took a buckboard to Daisy Conary's in Sunshine for a shore dinner, sometimes making a rendezvous with other parties under the awnings of her long, oilcloth-covered tables. Avoiding the mudflats in which the rig might easily bog down, the driver had to cross the ridge of sand close up against the beautiful red granite boulders of the Indian Causeway. At high water, sloops made the crossing without bothering to lift the centerboard.

The occasional trip to Stonington by buckboard was a very special

Fig. II-5. Crossing Scott's Bar to Little Deer Isle.

affair. The horses were rested up the whole day previous, for the granite-and-fishing town was so distant that a mutual distrust had existed for eons of time between its denizens and the inhabitants of our northern end of the island. There were the steep Southeast Hills to be negotiated, too, before the equipage rolled through neat elm-shaded South Deer Isle, and on through the white beauty of the birches that met over Lover's Lane. Several miles remained to be covered to the destination. It was not unusual for the more able-bodied males to hop out on the hills and spare the horses, who had to hold back hard against the rambling vehicle on the first of the pair, then made the arduous climb up the opposite slope. The sun was likely to be low on the horizon by the time the party returned.

But whenever one went—and there were less favored places—open to the sun above and never separated by glass or steel from nature, of which the buckboarder seemed peculiarly a part, blue August sky flecked with wisps of white clouds near above, he rejoiced in the steady clip-clop, the casual chat tuned to our pace, the freshly enthusiastic observation on some object by the roadside, the slow unfolding of the road ahead, the post-noontime fragrance of spruce and fir— Now one flits the twelve miles from end to end of the improved blacktop in under fifteen minutes—not merely once but twice or even three times a day, instead of perhaps once a summer. No tarrying at a roadside spring to water Dina and Maude from the S.P.C.A. pail—no time. No time either, homeward bound, to pick up the occasional neighbor glad to substitute

Fig. II-6. A stop to water the horses.

for plodding up the dusty road, a perch on the rear deck. One would be well past before recognizing him and besides, one would have to apply the brakes and shift gears! Alas, the high adventure of discovery has been supplanted by the boredom of the commonplace, and the humble buckboard, shining in its orange varnish, is but a memory to a few.

III

"He Maketh the Storm a Calm" (a backward look)

Fig. III-1. The farmhouse on Pickering Island, where the Scott family lived and the model for the story's farmhouse. Courtesy Deer Isle-Stonington Historical Society.

This story (never before published) grew out of a piece written by Captain Walter E. Scott (*Island Ad-Vantages* 12-13-62), who gave Tom permission to use "my great-grandmother's ghost story." A founder of the Deer Isle-Stonington Historical Society, Captain Scott was born in 1887, one of twenty-one children of John and Fannie Scott. When Walter was twelve, his family became caretakers of Pickering Island, living on the island by themselves through the winter. As a young man, Walter was a member of the crew of the *J. T. Morse*, soon going to Boston and serving from the freight deck to the pilothouse of all the steamers of the Eastern Steamship Company. In 1912, he became chief officer and alternating master of many of the sidewheelers and in 1914 was appointed as marine superintendant of the company. In this capacity, he had charge of all ships and their crews. In his later years, he wrote many letters for the local newspapers, several of which described the joys and hardships of living on Pickering Island.

☙ "He Maketh the Storm a Calm" (a backward look) ❧

All day long the wind had pounded the sea against the rocks of Fiddlehead, driving the rain before it in sheets that occasionally blotted out the trees on the little rocky promontory. She entered methodically in her diary:

> August 16, 1854. Heavy blow N.N.E. Joshie 3 days out.
> Everything is battened down here.

The island at such times was a particularly lonely spot. Take it on a sunny day when the bay was all aglitter and the gulls circled high against the blue, she did not mind that their little farm was completely surrounded by salt water and no other house stood by, but it did seem that those times when Joshie headed his schooner out for the Grand Banks or the Georges were over long and the layover between trips tantalizingly short.

As darkness closed in, the storm had reached gale proportions; though the staunch little shingled house sat low beneath a rise of ground, sheltered by the great spruces that crowned the hill, the windows rattled and an occasional puff sent a wisp of smoke out of the fireplace and into the room where she sat. And beneath it all, the steady pound, pound of the seas; sometimes it seemed that the very floor under her feet trembled with the reverberation. The rain had slacked off somewhat for the moment, so that when she opened the door onto the piazza, in the lee of their living room, she could catch dimly the revolving red sector of the beacon against the pitch black of the night. The very air tasted of salt spume, and she hurried back to the comfort of the flickering birch logs. Wherever the *Essie and Malcolm* might be, it must be miserable for those aboard her.

She had tucked little Saralyn early into her split-maple crib that Joshie had fashioned; the dishes were washed, the kitchen readied up, and the teakettle sang on the big black cookstove, which she had recently stuffed with chunks of pasture spruce. Now there was nothing to do but take up her quilting in the uncertain light of the fire and a single whale-oil lamp; best keep her fingers and her thoughts busy on a night like this. Oh, no question the *Essie and Malcolm* was able, had survived the test of many such gales as this, and Captain Joshua Weed everyone owned to be without a peer this side of Portland. She had been proud and flattered when he'd proposed at the end of a long courtship, and gave no second thought to leaving the warm comfort of the family hearth on Moose for Cap'n. Joshua's little island farm. Glory-be-to-Peter, they'd been neither one of them young, but where wouldn't she have followed that man!

She tossed a knotty piece of maple into the back of the fire and sat awhile, her fingers stilled, listening to the almost hypnotic ticking of the clock on the mantel. Yes, time had moved slowly, almost imperceptibly on; they had prospered, the farm was stocked with cattle and sheep and hens—and then, when they'd both just about given up hope, wee Saralyn had come to help fill the long intervals of her husband's absence at sea. The three of them had become very close in their little isolated home— she and Joshie and Saralyn. The child, with her cornflower eyes and golden hair, was the spittin' image of Mercy's baby pictures, Joshie said. Well, her own eyes were still cornflower and her hair still had its golden glints, and the wrinkles had not closed in yet about her mouth and eyes. Seemed like she and Joshie were so much one that distance had no power to separate them, really. There were times she called to mind when their thoughts crossed; arrived back on shore, he would corroborate a sudden sharp vision she had had or the shoreward flow of his thoughts. What did they call it, "mental telegraphy"? No need to fret, Mercy," he said. "If anything goes wrong with the vessel, which God forbid, you'll know it soon as I do." Now, the steady surf and the wailing of the wind intruded; indeed, they could never be quite shut out of her consciousness.

It was unquestionably as mean a night as she could recall. She was afraid there would be little sleep for her; the hands of the clock pointed toward eleven—long past her regular time for retiring. She picked up the family Bible from the corner of the parlor organ and turned to the Psalms, as her habit was. She had heard of devout souls somewhere, who in times of trouble, confronted by a fear or a question, had opened the Good Book without plan, placed a finger at random in the margin of the page that came up, and found opposite God's counsel. She hoped her faith in the Scriptures was no less; almost, for a moment, she thought of

Fig. III-2. Pogy House Cove on Pickering Island
(the story's "sand cove").

putting it to the test: "Is all well with Joshua and the men on the *Essie and Malcolm*, wherever they may be?"

Then, reluctantly, she turned back to the Psalms. Slim strips of paper and occasional scraps of ribbon marked many of her favorite passages, and she was soon following the words she found there, grateful for the shelter of her living room, while the clock ticked regularly, the logs crackled and hissed—the last one must have been a mite green still; maple sometimes took a lifetime to dry, seemed like—and occasionally a board creaked:

> Oh Lord how manifold are thy works! in wisdom hast thou made them all: the earth is full of thy riches.
>
> So is this great and wide sea, wherein are things creeping innumerable: both small and great beasts.
>
> There go the ships: there is that leviathan, whom thou hast made to play therein.

She could not have told how long she had been reading, when a particularly heavy gust, driving the rain before it, rattled the panes of the east window, drawing her eyes from their concentration on the book. From down in the direction of the sand cove a light appeared, following the little footpath, making its way slowly up across the field. Joshua! But not on a night like this; landing a small boat, even in the shelter of the cove was impossible. And no mortal would move so leisurely before the storm. Yet the light came on—flickering out, glowing wanly by turns. How could a candle lantern survive the elements? She recalled strange stories of her father's home on Moose—of how on occasion, coming back from the village store, he saw a candle light in the gable end, of his climbing to the attic, throwing open the door to find all dark, though he imagined he could hear the light tread of retreating footsteps and the creaking of the wide floorboards. She took hold of herself; this was no time to yield to fancy. Once more, she resumed her reading.

The knock on her kitchen door hardly came as a surprise, yet she sat in her chair close to the fire a full half minute till it was repeated—sharp, staccato, clear, unmistakable. And this time peremptory. She could no more have refused to respond to that summons than she could have stifled the vague fears that she was no longer able to deny. If not Joshie, it must concern Joshie. She flung the piazza door wide.

She was immediately aware of the rush of heavy, damp air across the threshold, of the intense saltiness of it, the smell of rockweed wrenched from the granite by a churning, angry sea. And she was aware, though the light of her whale-oil lamp had gone dim in the draft, of a vague figure, tall, though still lacking the stature of her husband, its narrow shoulders garbed in white, its head shrouded. The hand that reached toward her was chalky in the dim light—not skeletal, but somehow lacking in substance, cold as it touched her palm to deposit a piece of pigskin, completely dry despite the pelting of the elements. For some unaccountable reason, she knew no fear. Then the figure retired a step; it seemed to turn—or did it? Rather, in the dim light, it dissolved.

She stood there, for the moment transfixed, again aware of the pungent smell of kelp on barnacled rock, clutching the strange parchment. Then, mindless of the door open to the elements, she rushed back to the fireplace. Her lamp, burning blue in the draft, revealed an unfamiliar scrawl: "If your husband has met with disaster, the clock will stop at the hour of midnight." Once more, she scanned the message. She looked quickly at the mantel; the hands of the clock read seventeen minutes past eleven. Suddenly aware of the damp and the breath of the storm, she dropped the message on the little marble-topped table that held the lamp, strode back to the open door and slammed it shut. The back-draft swished the pigskin into the reaching fingers of the flames—but no matter, she'd read the strange characters twice. On the red-papered wall, three generations of seafaring Weeds looked sympathetically down at her from within their heavy frames. The horsehair sofa beckoned hospitably. Somehow she must dispel the dim forebodings, the unnamed fear; she must possess her soul with patience and put her faith in the Lord, though the messenger had seemed more like one sent by the Old Nick.

Resisting the sofa's blandishments and shielding the lamp with one hand, she carried it into the adjoining chamber. Saralyn had been restless—perhaps also, in her way, unable to shut out the menace of the storm. The room was chill, and she tucked the blanket tightly about one little shoulder that lay exposed. The child's breathing was even, now, and whatever had disturbed her bothered her no more. Mercy returned to the warmth she had left and set down the lamp, now burning yellow once more.

And once more she took up the family Bible. In the excitement, she had lost her place, but leafing methodically through the pages she found what she wanted again. She tried not to be aware of how sluggishly the hour hand on the shelf above her moved toward twelve. The print seemed uncommon small, even to her sharp eyes.

> They that go down to the sea in ships, that do business in the great waters; these see the works of the Lord, and his wonders of the deep. For he commandeth and raiseth the stormy wind which lifteth the waves thereof . . . they cry unto the Lord in their trouble, and he bringeth them out of their distress. He maketh the storm a calm, so that the waves thereof are still. Then are they . . .

The fall of the heavy Bible to the floor awoke her. The fire on the hearth burned low, and the room had grown unaccountably cold. Her mind was vaguely troubled—there had been something? Some message? Joshie! Her glance swept to the clock, still ticking inexorably away. The hands stood at three. It hadn't stopped, then. Thank God for that! To her ears, though the force of the storm seemed not to have appreciatively diminished, came the low, far-off blast of the horn on Hawk; the wind had veered round to the west. Tomorrow would be blue— Somewhat stiff, she returned to their chamber; without bothering to remove even her outer clothing, she dropped onto the bed next to the sleeping Saralyn, pulled the patchwork quilt over her shivering body and clear over her head as well.

಄ ಄

When the promise of the westerly breeze found realization in an almost cloudless morning, Mercy changed quickly into a fresh gingham dress, stuffed paper and kindling into the kitchen range, and started the fire. The fitted fir wood crackled deliciously and gave off a fragrance of which she never tired. With a dipper, she went out to the water barrel at the corner of the house. The Camden Hills loomed almost in her dooryard, and the gulls were mewing shrilly. As she leaned to scoop up a dishful of water, her eyes took note of footprints in the soft earth near the barrel. They were as wide and long as her husband's boot-jack—and they looked to have six toes. She could not say she was surprised; she was no longer worried, either. She made her way back to the sunny kitchen to boil Saralyn's eggs.

IV

Peanut, a Memory

F. P. Scott, also known as "Peanut," mentioned in "Leave by the Lower Deck, Forward," is the subject of this fictionalized account. His house and livery stable were just up the hill from the steamboat landing, across the road from the house of Charles Scott, Fred's "Cousin Charles." It was the house built originally by John Scott, who was the first to operate the Deer Isle Ferry. Although Charles' house still stands, Fred's was torn down in 1927. However, the barn survived for another three decades or so. Meredith Ellis, Charles' partner in the fish weir, lived in the house which is now the shop of Ronald Hayes Pearson. Originally part of the Scott holdings, this property passed to William Torrey, who married a daughter of Leonard Scott's sister. (Leonard, the second ferryman, was Charles Scott's grandfather.) William was the steamboat agent, whose nephew was Meredith Ellis. From Meredith, the property passed to his daughter, whose husband was Amos Scott, brother of Walter (see introduction to "He Maketh the Storm a Calm") and a cousin of Charles'. Thus was Scott ownership restored. Sam Knight, the ferryman, boarded with Charles Scott; his family lived in the house on Route 15 opposite the Lowe Road.

ଓ୫ Peanut, a Memory ଓ୫

FP Scott sat in the patent double lawn-swing in his front dooryard under the great horse chestnut tree that his father had planted and looked across at his cousin Charles' neat white clapboard house. It had been part of the old homestead once; sawed the end off, they had, and moved it onto its new cellar hole with oxen. It still left a sizeable house on the knoll behind him—gray and weather-beaten, with the siding hanging loose in places, windows cracked, one of its slender chimneys heeling crazily. The burdocks were crowding the orange lilies about the foundation, and the lilacs were gnarled and shabby. Why did it have to be that way, he wondered? And why had Charles and his family ostracized him goin' on twenty years? He couldn't remember, himself, what they'd fallen out about. Even the boy had turned his nose up at the beautiful little sloop Fred had carved to win his heart. "Go away you nasty old man." The boat lay broken where he threw it at his feet. Why did the island youngsters dog his footsteps, derisively shouting "Peanut!" And why did "Peanut!" on occasion make him angry enough to want to kill?

"Keish!"

And why did folks call him a miser? That was a good one! The neighborhood said he had money hidden in what remained of the cellar after his cousin's house had been severed. Now Charles—he raised his pale blue eyes to the freshly painted home across the road and the handsome orchard that lay below it, and so on out to the blue waters of the Reach beyond. Well, Charles, what with the motor ferry his father had rowed before him and the fish weir he and Meredith Ellis tended over by Carney Island, had plenty in the bank, you could be sure. Folks from all over the head of the island brought their checks to be cashed, fawned and called him captain, and voted for his choice at town meetings. All because he had a big balance at the Ellsworth Trust.

Somewhat ruefully, he surveyed his own domain—the old place, the home farm. And that's why Charles hated him, really—jealousy! Pah! To the left, his acres, spruce and fir swept down the hill to the road's intersection with the gravel cart-track down to the bar and over to Little Deer Isle. To the right, his fields strode up to the shore, providing hay for his two horses. His heart warmed as he thought of the black gelding and the brown mare in the drafty gray-shingled barn behind

Fig. IV-1. Fred Scott's house, overlooking the narrows of the Reach. Built by John Scott, the first ferryman; it was torn down in 1927.

him. Horses were better to get along with than most humans he knew. The black, now, would share a chaw from his Sickle Plug, nuzzle his shoulder, listen patiently, never mock him. To the black, he was F. P. Scott (never Peanut), owner of the only livery on the north end of the island.

The alders had crowded in down toward the water, but the little clearings there were carpeted with blueberries almost as big as grapes. Kept him busy chasin' the yowuns out, it did. Lord knows, he didn't begrudge them a few berries, but they tramped the vines. There was money in those berries, if he could only hack the alders down and keep the brush out; but a man could do just so much on a place, especially when, like as not, somebody'd call him out of the pasture to pick up a passenger clean up to the other end of the island. The brown horse was the best for the Southeast Hills on the long trip. And often, when he'd made the thirteen arduous miles, no passenger was waiting. Only derisive cries of, "Peanut, Peanut F. Peanut Scott!" "Keish! Git out a my blueberries!" the unseen voices mocked. He'd set about not going to Stonington anymore; but then, he couldn't afford not to go. When the call was genuine, it meant a dollar—and he needed the dollar as much as the next man. The livery men in the village, with their fancy rigs, charged two-fifty—and got it, too.

Those blueberries, now, if he could just give them the care they needed and, come they were ripe, if he had a dozen arms and hands!

When he'd tried to get pickers from over to Pinkeytown [Little Deer Isle] the miserable bastards had hidden water pails down in the alders and filled them up on the sly, sneaking them off home in their peapods. A poor sort! And most of the island folk wouldn't buy his berries, anyway. Said he was a dirty old man.

From his slatted seat in the swing, he saw the ferry set out from the main. Well, no time for musing. There'd be a passenger, maybe two. The advantage was his, seein's as he was on the spot and Tommy Gray's big horse livery was four miles off, in the village. With a protesting creak from the swing—and from his back (a body got stiff setting too long, by Godfrey! He was only three years younger than his cousin, and Charles was pushing sixty). He got up and went in to hitch up Old Black Sambo. The horse whinnied, genuinely glad to see him, and he patted the soft nose, running a hand over Sambo's side and down under his belly. "Good boy," he said. "*Somebody* loves the Old Man." He pulled down a little hay while he harnessed. Well, it would be a good fifteen minutes before the ferry made it to the ramp. Best rub up the brass on the harness a bit. As a final gesture, he took a grain bag down from off the floor and wiped the hen-daubin' from the back seat. Then he tossed a handful of grain down beside the barn door for the banty cock and his little harem, clambered into his hack and rattled down to the wharf.

The strange drummer making his way up the catwalk from the ferry took a careful look at the surrey with its moldy fringe, its greening upholstery with the three-cornered jags that let the stuffing leak through—a look that couldn't conceal his dislike at what he found.

"She ain't overly handsome, mister," Fred said. "But Gawdfrey mighty she's sound, and she'll get you to Northwest Harbor for twenty-five cents. You don't expect no landeau for that."

Fred flinched under the scrutiny of those unfriendly eyes that made him suddenly conscious of his unshaven face, the yellowed, tobacco-stained beard, the spotted serge suit, the blackened nails. "My God!" the drummer said, "Where can I telephone for a livery?"

There was nothing for Fred to do but drive old Sambo up the hill and unhitch. The experience was getting more and more common of late. It was close to supper time, he figured from the sun, so he watered the horses and got down an ample supply of grain, offering them soft cluck-ings and little words of endearment as he puttered about the stalls. Then he went back to the swing. When Sammy came stumping up the road on his one crutch after he'd snugged down the old double-ended *Suzie* at the float and thrown a tarpaulin over her five-horse make-and-break, Fred

Fig. IV-2. Sammy Knight, who ran one of the ferry's towboats.

was happy to see him turn in from the road and take the opposite seat. "Hi!" he said.

"Hi."

The little banty rooster on Fred's knee ruffled his feathers, then settled back, recognizing a friend. Sam might run the powerboat for Charles—one hundred percent loyal, he was, too—but he didn't plague Fred like the rest. In fact, just yesterday forenoon, when them young hellions loosened the nut from the axel on the off-hind wheel, so that as he started from the boat for the old gray barn the rig suddenly collapsed, it was Sam who put a stop to the taunting "Peanut! Hey Peanut!" and really gave them varmints what-for.

Sammy could rise into a temper mighty fast, all right. Many a time he'd seen it with his own eyes. Folks said, if 'twant for his crutch, Sammy'd be in the midst of any scrap within a mile of him. Seemed like when they was trouble, he automatically throwed in with the weaker side. Didn't give it a minute's thought. Come to think of it, maybe that's why Sammy took up with him. Well, they could say what they would about his temper; Fred had found him always gentle. Why, next to the horses, Sammy was his only friend.

It took some time to get around to what both men knew must ultimately be said. It was Fred who finally said it. "Sammy! Seems like I can't hardly make a go of it no more. The passengers I don't get is bad enough, but them yowuns is getting tarnation spleeny of late. And their elders puts 'em up to it. Do you know how it feels to be mocked? Sammy, I am a lonely man."

Sammy hadn't forgotten the boys' taunts back in his school days about his gimpy leg—not by a long shot. Yes he knew how it felt to be mocked. "Well, Fred, it's really what I stopped by to talk to you about."

"I cal'late they ain't much I can do about it now. It's gone on too long."

Sam hesitated, then took the plunge: "You ain't agoin' to like much what I've got to say."

Fred shifted his quid and spat wetly. "Sammy you can't hurt my feelin's more'n they've been today or yestiddy or day before that, I been sittin' here thinkin'."

"Fred, when did you change them clothes last?"

"Back in April, deah. Come spring I allus get into a fresh set of flannel underwear and my summer suit."

"I thought as much, and excuse me if I'm just a mite personal, but did you have ye a bath then?"

Fred hedged. "Sammy did you ever try standin' in a tin tub in a house that ain't got proper heat and the wind blowin' through the cracks and tried to soap in half a pail of tepid water, while you saved the other half to rinse with? I've got out of the way of it."

"Plenty's done it . . . You know what folks are sayin'? 'My boy Nealie sneaked up and peeked into the old skinflint's window t'other day, and what do you suppose? The cook-room was piled up with all sorts of clutter and the sink full of dishes that ain't been washed for weeks!' . . . Don't interrupt me, Fred, I'm only tellin' what they say. 'And on the table my boy sees a soup dish Peanut's been eatin' stew out of; he ain't never washed it, and it's all crusted in from the edges till there's only a little hole in the middle, size of an egg, to eat out of!' And they say you use your horse stalls for a privy—"

Fred whittled a chaw from his Sickle Plug and added it to his quid. "If they're good enough for the horses—"

Sam started the swing gently in motion. The little cock teetered on his perch, dug his nails into the knee of the blue pants; Fred ruffled the feathers of his neck with a gentle hand.

"That two-seater, Fred, how long you had it?"

"Since the winter you and Charles come nigh to freezing yourselves bringin' the mail 'cross, through the drift ice. You was just a yowun then. I'd say about twenty-five years."

Sam shifted his gimpy leg and propelled the swing gently with his crutch. "Fred, I'll tell you . . . You take it, a man begins to pinch his pennies, folks start to mock him . . . 'specially if they ain't got many

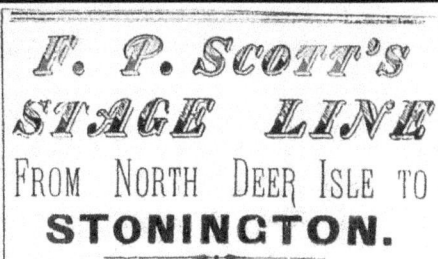

Fig. IV-3. This ad for F. P. Scott's Stage Line is from the September 7, 1901, issue of *The Island Press*. Courtesy Deer Isle-Stonington Historical Society.

pennies themselves. And when he lets himself go to seed like—well, they lose their respect for him, particularly since he seems to have lost his own."

Fred spat again, the yellow saliva dripping down his beard. "Ayuh," he said.

"Now I'll tell you what; you got to make a new start, like. You go down on your sand beach—won't nobody see you down there—and strip off. You take it on the flood tide, and that water's not too cold, coming up over them flats warmed by the sun like it does. Fetch some fresh clothes down along and burn them you got on, from the skin out . . . And that hack of yours, all tattered and spotted, with them rumblin' wheels . . . Why don't you get you a new rubber-tired surrey?"

"Keish," Fred said, "you must think I'm a rich man, Sammy."

"I don't, neither. I'm tellin' you what you got to do. Maybe it ain't too late; anyways, you can't go on like this."

The vision grew: the new shiny, rubber-tired surrey, his neighbors proud to speak to him now— He hugged the picture close. The lawn swing became some new-fangled sort of flying-machine, soaring with him into the blue. "And Keish, Sammy, I'll get me a frock coat, a derby and yellow gloves for taking out the rusticators on a Sunday."

Lizzie blew a blast on the conch shell to call Sam home for supper.

Before boat time next day, Fred crouched on the float beside the ferry, while Sam tinkered with an igniter. The bright vision of the previous evening had faded. "I been thinkin', Sammy, about yestiddy; Sammy, I can't do it."

The ferryman reached for his crutch from the floor of the cockpit and pulled himself erect. His face grew red. "Why in tarnation's name can't you Fred?"

"Now don't you be getting mad at me, deah! Honest, Sammy, I ain't got the money!"

"When you talk that way, I'm deef as a halibut! You ain't as rich as some folks say, but you got enough. Who you goin't to leave it to when you die—Charles? He's your nearest kin."

He hadn't figured it that way; the thought brought him up short. "Well, anyway, them horses, Sammy, they ain't as young as they used to be. If I got me this new rig, my business'd mebbe grow to the point where them critters'd be pooched, what with all that extra runnin'. I love them horses, Sammy, and I wouldn't no more want to overwork 'em than I would have my old mother."

"King-darn-it, Fred, sometimes I feel's if I could take you by the shoulders and shake you till your teeth rattled!" Sam's sudden anger vanished as quickly as it had come. "Now, we got this all settled once. You can't go and change your mind like this. Don't you worry about them horses none; plenty of life in the old cayuses yet. And how do you know they ain't downright embarrassed at pullin' that old thing around after them. You got to make folks respect you, understand?"

"But Sammy them horses—"

Sam pointed to the rail above them, where two shock-headed boys in overalls were busy lashing the wheels of Fred's old two-seater with a spare length of painter while the brown mare looked back with languid eyes.

"Keish! You boys clear out from there!" Fred hurried up the long catwalk, shouting imprecations as he went, to which Sam added full measure from the float.

CB CR

When the surrey came off the Maine Central Boat, its upholstery tightly buttoned, freshly blue, a beautiful thing from another world, Fred could hardly believe the reality of his situation himself. He nudged Sam delightedly in the ribs. "Consigned to Fred P. Scott," the purser announced to the agent.

Where he stood, off in the shadow of the little square office, Fred was aware of the hum of surprise and admiration. He was aware of another hum, as Sam pushed him gently into the circle of light at the head of the slip—a gray little man, conscious of his new haircut, his freshly shaven face, the new double-breasted suit—to claim his new possession. "My God, Fred," the agent said, "what happened? Someone die and leave you a mint?"

Others were gathered round the carriage. Fred felt himself expand as he joined them. "Thought it's about time I modernized my equipment," he observed to the group at large. He expounded on the virtues of the rig.

"A slick little cutter." Elwyn Hardy was unable to conceal his admiration. And it was "Fred this and Fred that"; no longer was it "Peanut." The new day had arrived.

By some miracle, Fred felt, he'd rejoined the human race. "I'd appreciate it," he told them, "if you'd feel free to recommend my livery to your friends."

Even the horses seemed to be impressed with their new status in the community and stepped higher in consequence in the days that followed. Their harnesses gleamed with oil and polished brass. Fred reserved the silk hat for very special occasions. But gradually he became aware of another change in his neighbors, though he could not exactly name it. He could not know that now some were saying, "The little upstart, who does he think he is!" "Putting on all them airs!" "Why, we knew him when he looked like something the cat dragged in." "So the old miser has managed to tear himself loose from a few of his dirty dollars, has he?" The boys had stopped plaguing him, but it seemed an uneasy truce.

"You know," Sam told him, "maybe you're layin' it on a mite thick. I'd put aside that derby hat for a while."

"Could be, you're right," Fred said, "but I'm picking up the first selectman at the wharf tonight, and he might be hurt if he was the first I didn't wear it for— Believe me, Sammy, I appreciate your advice and all you've done for me no end. Why, you've changed my whole life."

No other rigs came for the night boat; any passengers were likely to be strictly local, still not too tired from their day in Rockland to walk the short distance home. Fred roamed about the wharf till boat time, pausing to exchange a word here and there about crops and the weather, no longer a man alone. Behind the freight house he came upon some of the boys pushing about Charles' two-wheeled mail cart. It didn't matter now that he and this cousin hadn't exchanged a word in twenty years; as a repatriated social being, he rose to his responsibilities: "Keish boys, have a care with that cart; a little more and you'll have her over the side."

An apple flew through the air and hit the derby hat square; there was a splash as it landed below. And there rose again that half-forgotten battle cry, "Peanut! F. Peanut Scott!"

Something long dormant rose within him. He seized the biggest and nearest of his tormentors by the sweater and delivered a solid crack across the side of a face he could not see. "You gosh darn jackasses, you!" The boy went whimpering off.

Before he had finished his business there and rounded the freight house, hatless, a little knot of men confronted him, Sam stumping in the lead, leaning heavily on his single crutch. "You big brute," Sam stuttered in his anger. "And I've tried to be your friend. What do you mean by striking that innocent boy!" You always hated Charles; now, by God, you have to take it out on his son." The others grouped menacingly at Sam's back.

"But, Sammy—" The futility of his whole struggle pressed suddenly upon him. Somehow, this one man—his true friend—must be made to understand. In his eagerness, his voice rose shrilly: "But, Sammy! You don't understand! Them yowuns—"

"We'll hear no more about it. A man grown, striking a small boy! And not much of a man at that. If—"

But F. P. Scott didn't hear the rest. Sammy! All he could do was go bury his face in the black gelding's neck. When the horse whinnied, and nuzzled him softly, upper lip pulled back, Fred sliced him off an extra-size chaw of Sickle Plug.

The next day, he was unshaven, collarless, and the first spots appeared on the new double-breasted jacket.

V

No Good 'Thout a Woman

Published in *The General Magazine and Historical Chronicle* in 1952 (volume LIV, No. III pages 153-158), this is a highly embroidered account that stems from an actual incident. As the saying goes, "the names of the characters have been changed to protect the innocent."

○○ No Good 'Thout a Woman ○○

Amos looked up from the Sears big midsummer catalogue, which the rural delivery man had just left him. He wasn't much of a hand for talking, and, brief as it had been, their conversation was finished. "I just got to think it all through, Sam," he said.

A clash of gears and Sam Pickering had eased his battered "Chevvie" on toward the next farm. Back in the doorway of the big white barn, Amos took up again his whittling on a pinkie rig. One massive hand, its knuckles prominent from twenty years of hauling on to ropes, held the little craft poised delicately; his placid face was knit in a frown of concentration. Somehow, a knife and a block of pine could help a man's thoughts run freer.

No use ownin' he wa'n't thankful that when the end come, old Nelse had slipped his moorinn's easy. A true Torrey, his father—no crazy notions about death; and come to that, precious little time for undertakers. "They ain't no need in fillin' a body full o' chemicals," Sam reported old Nelse had said at the last; "I want that Amos should plug my nose and ears solid with cotton battin' and give me a coat o' copper paint from stem to stern. You take it on a ship's bottom, now; they ain't nothin' better t' stop her from foulin', an' to keep the worms out."

Amos smiled wryly. Even if he'd been a mind to carry out his father's orders, the *Annie and Reuben* had warped her broad beam up to the clam factory wharf just ten days too late— Knocking about, up and down the coast under sail, you lost touch with things. Only dimly aware of the munching of the cattle, the clanking of their halter chains, and their gentle lurchings against the side of the stalls as they ate, he faced his altered future. No use thinkin' on the sea. The sea! Folks—particularly the women folks—liked to plague him with it. "His only mistress," they said with a sly leer. Worst of 't was, they was right; he wa'n't no hand with the women. Hadn't ever been—clean back when he was a yowun. Whenever the Grange or the Blue Lodge or the Rockbound Rebeccas had them a time in the hall over the Town House, he was one o' the crew that stood in the doorway an' watched with sheep's eyes an' twisted his handkerchief into a hard knot. And come the time the others had got a holt on their courage when the fiddles took up "Merchant's Island," and they was balancing pa'tners in the Lady of the Lake, or stompin' down the center in a way to set the faded pink crepe streamers that festooned the ceiling all atremble, he stole outside onto the mill dam and looked up at the stars or out across the empty harbor—looked and ate his heart out! It wa'n't as if he didn't care. King-darn-it no!

And for a good many years a-runnin' now, it was the same. He'd seen the trim ones married first—Doris and Genice and Norma—and then, one by one, nigh on to all the rest, sweet- and ugly-tempered alike. And whenever anything in calico to the lee side of fifty hove to, he was dumb as a halibut—all weak-like inside.

With one quick stroke, Amos slashed the pinkie rig amidships and dropped it into the litter at his feet. He couldn't dodge the issue any longer. "Ayuh, I'm a farmer now, and a farm's no good 'thout a woman." He snapped the knife shut abruptly, cast an appraising glance at the fog rolling in over the hackmatacks by the pasture wall, and went in to bed down the cattle.

ଓ ଔ

Come Saturday, Sam and Amos took the sooty little *Pemaquid* over to Rockland, and Amos had him some cabinet photographs in the double-

Fig. V-1. A saltwater farm on Deer Isle, this one established by Joseph Smith Greenlaw in 1836.

breasted blue serge folks allowed made him look like a master in steam. Even if his Adam's apple was a mite prominent in a wing collar—when a body don't wear a collar everyday, they like plenty room—he had to own the result wa'n't too bad; the handsome waterfall he'd coaxed into the hair over his forehead, his face without a line 'ceptin' for them little creases round the eyes that come from long, bright days at sea, the jaw that'd showed it could take anything short of a belayin' pin— And his big mustache covered up where he'd lost them three front teeth in a little affair with a contrary crew off Barbados— Tough, them Jamaica niggers, bad seamen—and treacherous.

The folks in the studio'd wanted to tint the order—said, nay, you take a man with his ruddy face and them china blue eyes, they allus looked right smart tinted. Well, he couldn't afford it, and he figgered this'd have to do.

Back home, Amos lost no time dropping the photos off in several quarters on the south end of the island and letting folks know his mind. "You see, I'm cal'latin' to take a partner"—his attempt to be casual sounded hollow even in his own ears. "I don't set much store by these young things, as wanta be runnin' all day, an' dancin' the Portland Fancy half the night. I ain't got time for any such foolishness. What I need's an active sort of cutter, as can tend the stock and look after the hens. Maybe you might know a likely woman?"

It was Sam Pickering brought Amos views about the woman from away, working for Annie-Liz at the boarding house in the village. That was Tuesday forenoon. Thursday the red flag was up on Amos' mail box, and Sam stopped. Sitting in his accustomed spot, Amos looked up from his whittling, to where the Camden Hills loomed blue across the bay. "That woman at The Ark, Sam . . . I was down yestiddy. I pulls the bell, and then I wisht ta God I hadn't. B'um'bye she came to the door. My face feels like a boiled lobster, but I 'lows as to how I want to be 'quainted with 'er."

Sam nodded.

"So we goes into the cook-room, where she's ironin', an' me in mortal terror Annie-Liz'll make soundin's any minute and want to know what an old he-goat like me is doin' of in the galley."

Sam watched the chips fall with mathematical precision from the knife blade to the splintered pine plank.

"Well, we talks about the weather, an' how she likes here compared to over on the main. Pretty slick cutter from the looks of 'er, and it don't take a sculpin's eye t' see she's a good hand at pressin' a shirt, nuther. They's a kettle o' chowder on the back of the stove. Sam, I know my fish chowder, and by-Godfrey-Damon this one smells prime!

"So I goes on, from the weather to the farm—the acre o' potatoes, and the cukes, the blueb'ry pasture, an' the Early Astrachans. An I got a couple cows, I tells 'er, an' a pig, an' a flock 'o barred Plymouth Rocks! Sam, it's devilish hard goin'. Then I takes another good sniff o' that chowder, an' I swallows hard. An' then, Sam I done it! How'd you like to come up-along to my place?" I says.

"How much wages you 'lowin' to pay?" she says.

"Wages!" I says. "I wa'n't figgerin' no wages. I aims to marry up with ye.

"Well, sir, I cal'late it was sudden-like. While she's a-turnin' of it over in her mind, I kinda runs a weather eye over her spars. And by King, Sam, if the critter ain't got 'er a wooden leg."

Sam's low whistle of surprise seemed to call for further explanation.

"Ayuh! A wooden leg. I mind she walked kinda stiff-like when she come to the front door. So I says right off quick, "Well, you ain't eager, I can see that. We'll just forget it!" An' I puts."

Sam made commiserating noises as he threw old Betsy into gear. But two weeks later he was inclined to see the finger of Providence in the whole affair.

That was when he and Isophenie were just about fed up with ten days of Ida-Margaret. Ida'd turned up in the cook room one evening, bag and baggage, just as Isophenie was bringing a pan of curds from down cellar for supper. "It's so cold over to the Cranberry Isles in the wintertime," she announced in her harsh, masculine voice, "what with bein' right out t' sea, you might say, an' th' salt spume freezin' on th' window-panes, that I says to Litha-Norine"—gripping a plain, tow-headed youngster more firmly by the hand—"sez, 'Now your father's dead, I'll not put in another winter on them God-forsaken rocks!'" She drew in deeply and noisily of the fragrance from the array of kettles steaming on the woodstove and cast an eye over the day's pack of pickles and preserves standing topside down on the long maple dresser. "I know it's a mite early, Cousin Sam'l, but no harm in bein' forehanded, I always say; I've come to spend the winter with you and Isophenie."

Sam allowed later that Ida-Margaret took a grip on that household like the Old Man of the Sea: "Always in the best patent rocker, the one that used t' play 'Rollin Down t' Rio' when a body sat in it—and her big enough to swamp a Gloucester dory. Wonder she hadn't pooched the thing outright."

Isophenie could stand just so much. "I tell you, Sam, what with her appetite, that woman'll have us on the town 'fore winter's out. She's your kin; now you c'n just git shet of her."

It was then Sam's eye fell athwart Amos' cabinet photograph on the shelf of the parlor organ. He laid aside the weekly *Messenger*, knocked the ashes out of his pipe, and set out up the road.

"Amos," he said, when he finally ran down his quarry dumping a mess of turnips into the pig's trough by lantern light, "we've got a widdy-woman up to our place I'd like you to see. She's a leetle on the meaty side, mebbe, but she's active, and sma't as a steel trap." He'd have to make it sound good; it was no secret to the whole head of the island that Amos had just turned over the back chamber to a woman from over by Keezar Mountain, on trial.

"You tidy up a bit," Sam counseled; "set the cordwood out of the front pa'lor an' clean them hen-daubins off'n th' sofa, and I'll fetch 'er down to visit with ye."

༼ཨ༽   ༼ཨ༽

Ida-Margaret took to the farm from the moment she saw the big Star Kineo in the kitchen, the ample wood-box, and the iron sink with its copper pump. And she owned to Isophenie, confidentially, that she

Fig. V-2. Deer Isle's "church on the hill."

admired Amos' big red mustache. It showed a man was virile. So she and Litha-Norine took over the front chamber, and he had to be content with the haircloth sofa under the whatnot in the freshly swept front parlor.

Amos didn't find the arrangement too satisfactory. "Ayuh, I like to take my comfort," he lamented to Sam. "I can't figger where that sofa got all them knobs in it, and the dod-gummed thing so slippery I've slid off it now two nights runnin' and brought up on the floor all-standin', and all the time them two women at it like a couple o' bobcats."

Amos admitted to being downright pleased when the candidate from Keezar Mountain evacuated the back chamber, decamping with a snug-haired kitten and her rival's only pair of rayon stockings. "They got 'em out to Sears," Amos placated Ida-Margaret; "sixty-nine cents, an' ring-free, it says, though what that is I don't know."

While he was at it, by way of surprise, Amos explored the more intimate sections of the big catalogue—some o' them pictures made a man blush, outright—and ordered somethin' sma't enough, what with the bow on the bosom and that handsome lace at the bottom, to wear to town meetin' or lead the march-in-circle in. A slip, they called it. He had to own to being a mite uncertain about the size.

"A man's kinda shy in female matters," he confided to Ida, as they opened the package together. "I didn't just like to ask ye, but I got it plenty big. And now if it fits ye, I'll just get into a clean pair o' dungarees, and maybe we mought look up Pa'son Eaton—that is, if ye feel up to walkin' to the Ha'bor. 'Tain't more'n five mile, dead reckonin'."

In the small, white parsonage next to the "church on the hill," they were effectively spliced. "Not like I heard it done on shipboard once, when one o' the hands got in a little trouble down to Trinidad, and she stowed away in the longboat." He tugged at his long mustache. "But nice language," he agreed.

Amos passed out Pippins to his neighbors—five cents straight, but he wanted to do the thing up right. And he dropped in on some of the summer people with his bride. "Standin' there, front o' th' preacher, in that white slip an' a white veil, she had looked just like an angel—" He paused for a moment to enjoy the rather ample vision in retrospect, then continued in his easy drawl, "I didn't know but what if you had any washin', you mightn't want this woman t' do it." And he made the rounds, prudently collecting the cabinet photographs from where they reposed on tasseled mantels, or on whatnots along with the wax fruit and the rosy pink shells full of the sound of China seas.

"Ayuh, no use in leavin' 'em to collect dust," he said. "I'll just take 'em home-along. Besides, sometimes the papers want pictures—the owner of the best-pullin' yoke of oxen at Bangor Fair, of who has the Boston Post's cane as the oldest man on the island, an' whatnot. Might be, too, this woman'd die, though the Lord forbid, and I'd want to sign me on another mate. A farm's no good 'thout a woman. I'll keep 'em by."

It seemed right to Amos that their honeymoon was spent raking late blueberries from among the junipers and alders in the shore pasture. Gulls soaring overhead, the rote of the tide on the rocky shore, and the bay sparkling blue beyond—the new life and the old! And all to the accompaniment of a succession of blue'bry pies—as plump as the new partner, herself. No one was more surprised than Amos at the change from his usual shy self. He glowed with happiness. "By Godfrey, it makes me downright sick to think what I been missin' all these years."

The neighbor women, rocking at their kitchen windows, seeing the two of an afternoon, hand in hand on the dusty road to the ferry landing, waved a greeting. It was all part of the new life to him; he could not hear them sigh, "Poor Amos, she's a homely critter, but he's waited so long he's a right to be happy." All he knew was that the old shyness that had tortured him time out of mind had scaled like an early morning fog.

When Litha-Norine's sister arrived, Amos didn't give much thought to it; a slow man, he wasn't one to talk. But as Ida-Margaret began reassembling her brood, of which he'd had no past knowledge, scattered in orphanages and homes, he couldn't help from observing in confidence to Sam that, if not promiscuous, his mate had been at least prolific. For awhile there seemed no end.

"How many yowuns be they got? Now, let's see . . ." Ida-Margaret counted slowly on her thick, stubby fingers, "There's Charlene and Maxine and Rose-Genice and Gwenevere-Evangeline and Izora-May . . ." Eyes shut, heavy features set in the effort, she became lost in her computations.

"And not a boy in the lot," Amos said. Did his voice take on just a touch of bitterness, or did Sam imagine it?

☙ ☙

He don't feel so smart here of late, Amos confesses; likes to sit out in the sunshine by the barn door. Talks quite a lot about the old *Annie and Reuben*. "Now there was a trim vessel, and a free traveler 'fore the wind. Why, I mind the time, off the Georges . . . Farmin'? Well, a body has to keep active to feed a family size o' this. Ayuh. And the way the weeds spring up overnight's a caution."

Marriage does seem to take it out of a man, too. Not that he'd say a word 'gainst matrimony, understand . . . The boys in the neighborhood keep an eye peeled for mullein weed—a mess of it over by the old marble quarry down the Reach; you take it, with some skunk-cabbage root, and brew it into a tea, like, and they ain't nothin' can touch it for the miseries of any kind.

Sam owns to being concerned about Amos. "I'm afraid he's losin' his courage," he opines. "Bad thing when a man loses his courage. Now you take the other day. I come on him tendin' a brush fire by the rock pile at the far end of the orchard. Just as I heaves in sight he tosses on a passel o' somethin'. 'Course I can't say for certain, from where I stands, looks mighty like it might be them cabinet photographs."

VI

Home for Christmas

Another piece of fiction, in this case wholly made up, as far as we know. We recall no incident like this one related here, though it may be we just never heard of it. All the names and places are fictional. The story is published here for the first time.

ა Home for Christmas ა

Miss Mattie's stately white house with its chimneys at either end, its green blinds and its lovely fanlight doorway had lain empty on its hillside since the day the selectmen had come to take her up to Bangor. Yet, though the old semi-formal garden in which it was set was overgrown and fallen into disarray, it still bore the unmistakable stamp of the patrician.

"Queer" in these latter years, after her husband's death, she subsisted with a few hens and a vegetable garden which Reuben turned up for her early each spring. Just how she supported that stooped and emaciated form, no one rightly knew; for the past five years, she had not stirred beyond her dooryard. There were those who said that her beagle brought her rabbits and squirrels for the stew pot, but that was hard to credit, for the dog was old and rheumatic. Those who called, either through kindness or curiosity, found themselves rebuffed: "No need to worry about me, my dears. And I'm sorry not to invite you in, but you see, I haven't had time to tidy up since the big party last evening. So we'll just have to stand here on the stoop. Oh, it was an occasion, I'll tell you, with some of the finest folks in town come for good conversation and a glass o' wine. Why there was…" And the visitors felt their flesh creep a bit as she recounted details drawn from parties long past, when her sea-captain husband, famed for his hospitality, and for his Madeira which had twice rounded the Horn, had entertained the elite of the neighborhood. Many of the names she dropped were of townsfolk who had paid their last debt to life and passed on to a dubious reward. The town fathers did not get her across the doorsill and into the car without a struggle.

As for Miss Mattie's house, it settled back for a long slumber. Though it was once set high and surrounded by rose beds, syringas, lilacs and other shrubs, its cedar hedge, no longer kept in bounds by periodic trimming, and a new growth of pasture fir and spruce obscured it from the road. Had there been neighbors nearer than a half a mile, they would not have missed the thin wraiths of smoke curling from its chimneys by day, or the dim glow of its kerosene lamps by night. The phone and electricity had been disconnected long since. Country boys are less cruel to an old house than their city cousins, so that only two or three of the small panes were missing from their sash. Few travelers passed that way, for the blacktop ended a mile short of the old mansion, at the last little cluster of houses, and since the unimproved portion no longer offered a navigable shortcut to Ship's Cove, there was nothing to draw other than an occasional exploratory car down this way.

Sometimes, one of the more venturesome of the summer folk who had heard snatches of the tale of Miss Mattie ventured to peer through the sleeping house's cracked and putty-less windows. It was the birthing room, just off the kitchen, which she had taken over as the years brought their weight to bear against her. Those who had taken her away, impelled by some sense of what was decent, had pulled the patchwork quilt up over the unoccupied bed and tidied the chamber up a mite, man fashion; the effect was of the owner's continued presence—a flowered cotton dress thrown over the ladder-back chair, a woolen nightgown draped over a post of the spool bed, a book opened face-down on the little bedside table, a clutter of combs and half-empty perfume bottles on the bureau's marble top.

The adjoining kitchen that had once extended its warmth to the beginning of life rather than its declining years, with its array of antique iron and copper utensils, its drop-leaf table still bearing the staples of a forgotten meal, made those who peeked through its curtain-less windows drool. From the dining room which flanked it on the other side, the family silver had been removed for safe keeping, at the behest of a wholly unknown great-grandniece on the West coast, but the gracious paneled room and its contents were otherwise intact. Chairs slumbered at a gleaming mahogany table still extended by several leaves, which bore witness to the grand dinners of yore. Corner cabinets were still stocked with fine old china—medallion and Canton ware—the massive Georgian sideboard concealed a rich supply of linens; a still-life was highlighted by a beam of the sun: a bowl of luscious fruits and a pheasant yet unplucked, its head hanging in death from the table which held them.

Those intruders upon the sleeping hours here, who moved to the piazza to pry into the secrets of the drawing room, were rewarded with shelves of books, many of them richly bound, in cavernous mahogany cases on either side of the open hearth with its graceful mantelpiece of Italian marble. Except for the droppings of chimney swallows on the hearth, the room had not gathered appreciable dirt. A large copper kettle held logs to supplement the birch that waited, ready for the match, on the andirons. On the splendid old mahogany tower desk, where the captain had kept the record of his prosperity at sea, still lay his sextant, a chart, binoculars, which Miss Mattie had never allowed to be disturbed.

All of this left to the guardianship of the trees and the rutted land. "Criminal!" said the growing colony of summer folks: an authentic eighteenth-century colonial, which some fortunate one should be permitted to restore, with anchors cut in solid shutters and carriage lamps set on either side of its heavy-paneled front door. And the furniture! Why, there were things in this moldering old house worth a small fortune. It was definitely antisocial not to put them into circulation through some neighboring dealer in antiques!

As for Miss Mattie, sixty miles away: she was bathed regularly, well cared for, well fed (the meager old body even showed vague signs of plumping up a bit); unquestionably, the State Hospital was the place for her. Of course, she kept talking of going home, but most of them did that occasionally—didn't know what was really best for them. Ridiculous in her case, utterly unable to care for herself in that damp old barrack, her head full of its silly fancies! She gave them no trouble in her new home but remained a solitary. "Difficult, of course," the supervising psychiatrist said, "to break the habit of years. At present, she resists all our efforts to interest her in the normal things: cards, puzzles, TV." The second year was like the first, the third like its predecessors. "I must get along home," she said.

"But, Miss Mattie, there's nobody there anymore. You must remember, dear, your husband—the man you married—is no longer living."

"Not Warren," she said. "I didn't marry him; I married the house . . ." Strange what a poor twisted brain could conjure up. As if one could marry a *house*!

Of course, technically, the house belonged to the town now; it was common knowledge that Miss Mattie had paid no taxes for some years before they took her up to Bangor. The cost of her keep had been growing, and the pressure upon the selectmen as well. More and more folks, mostly from away, had approached them to covet this or preempt that, including the house itself. And besides, it does a building no good to shut it up tight, particularly if its cellar is always damp, come spring. The sills were going, the roof needed attention. While it had been easier—and cheaper—just to let Mattie stay on than establish her on a poor farm, the time to take action on the house had finally come, preferably before the new year.

The selectmen felt the duty of informing her of the move, though, heaven knew, they had no relish for the job. Their visit to Bangor opened pleasantly enough with the news of town doings; Miss Mattie seemed genuinely glad to see them. In some ways, it made the job more difficult. Well, they could dodge the issue no longer. "Miss Mattie," the head of the delegation said, "you always was a sensible sort of body with a proper feeling for the town. Now that you're comfortable and happy here, we've got to think of the expense the town is under for your keep."

"Ephraim, it was none of my choosin'," she said.

"No. But it seemed the only possible answer to your situation—where you'd get fittin' care, and all. Of course, according to the books, with your taxes unpaid all these years, the house really belongs to the town. But we're hopin' you'll want to turn it over yourself, to help repay—"

She stopped him with an imperious gesture: "I'll never!"

"But, Miss Mattie, let's be sensible—"

"Ephraim, I *am* sensible. I don't like it here. This year I mean to spend Christmas at home!"

☙ ❧

The light, downy flakes through which she had trudged the last several hours had given way to a stinging, icy blizzard as she turned the button on the storm door of the back shed and, slipping inside, groped clumsily about the top of one of the studs where it met the cap piece. Her hands were quite numb and her body, in its light cloth coat, chilled almost beyond feeling; but tenaciously she persisted, and sure enough, there the spare key was, safely concealed, as always. She inserted it with difficulty into the lock and the kitchen door swung open with a protesting creak. A gust of stale air, damp and heavy with memories of the past, greeted her. She swung the door to behind her and sank exhausted into the patent rocker by the big woodstove, but with a sigh of satisfaction. She was home! The poor bemused brain was not capable of thinking how clever she had been to cover the miles that lay between Bangor and home without money, guided by only that instinctive sense of the homing pigeon. Nobody would refuse a ride to an old woman on such a night as this, especially Christmas Eve. She had the vaguest memory of the several lifts involved and of kind, solicitous faces. She had discouraged all conversation, offered nothing herself beyond the fact that she was coming home for Christmas. Now, for a time, in the chilly house, she sank into a bemused slumber, from which she stirred occasionally, to be aroused at last by a vague sense of where she was.

She awoke in the pitch dark, still chilled but less benumbed. Almost instinctively she moved to the wood-box, found the kerosene can nearby, lifted the lid on the old King Clarion and, though her fumblings were pitiful even to her, kindled the spruce chunks that she'd always kept laid there, then sank back again exhausted by her effort. Slowly the room became less chill, then vaguely warm—her own movements less stiff. She found an oil lamp on the shelf behind the stove, turned up the wick and set a match to it. Then, with slow, methodical steps, carrying the lamp before her, shielding her eyes from its glow, she made her way into the drawing room and lighted the big lamp with the rose-covered china shade. She smiled with satisfaction; everything was as she remembered it from the day Warren had brought her home as a bride: the heavy pink drapes, the portraits of his father and mother looking severely down from the wall, the dusty model of a brigantine upon the mantel shelf, the large tinted photograph of his first wife on the drum table. The doors that gave access to the rest of the house were closed, and already a faint touch of heat slipped in from the kitchen she had left.

It called for considerable more effort now by her poor old back and her stiff limbs to reach down and ignite the kindling beneath the four sturdy pieces of birch waiting on the half-anchor andirons; the bark kindled quickly, and the logs shortly settled down to a satisfying roar. Her body responded gratefully to this new source of comfort, but the chill was deep-seated within her. From far off a thought suggested itself to her. The half-gallon jug—the jug of rum that Warren had always kept against emergencies, in a dark corner at the top of the cellar stairs. Her movements were easier now. She opened the door, lifted down the jug, partly filled the tumbler which was kept inverted over its neck. She took a sip, then a long swallow; the fire raced through her veins. She upended a couple more two-foot lengths and dropped them onto those already blazing on the hearth. She tugged the old leather rocker to a spot directly in front of the blaze, sloughed off her long coat and settled back, almost lost in the chair's cavernous depths. Another half glass of the brandy made smooth with the years and her comfort was complete. Her eyes drooped.

This room, which had been for so long the center of her life, sharer of hopes, receiver of confidences, took her again into its embrace. The dancing flames brought the walls in close, with their paper in formal designs slightly faded, which family tradition said had been brought in from the East in a tea clipper by one of Warren's forebears; they highlighted things familiar and long loved—the little brigantine, the family portraits, the painting of the whale tossing the three ship's boats in the shadow of an iceberg, swinging his tail and spouting mightily.

The poor old eyes closed for a time, as she settled back in the rocker. Dreams, fantasies, memories—she could not be certain which was which—passed in long procession through her troubled mind. The drawers of the drum table contained many treasures. No need to lock it now. Almost as one walking in her sleep, she made her way to it and withdrew sheaves of papers, ribbons, letters, mementos from its drawers, fetching them back to her rocker. She'd married the captain well into her middle years; this trove represented her long vanished youth that even Warren could not know. How often, when he was off to sea, she'd spread them in her lap as she did now: pink and blue hair ribbons from special occasions, a certificate to Miss Mattie Sylvester for special skill in Spenserian exercises, signed by the district superintendant—and the book itself, with its whirls, its intricately inked designs, its Spenserian birds, its letters perfectly formed . . . These elbow-length white kid gloves—they'd gone with the beautiful long white dress all buttonholed, especially got for the musical evening at the Congo Church. Her performance had been "a dramatic triumph," her friends had told her. There was this girl whose mother has died, and she sings this terribly pathetic song. How did it go?

> Hello Central, give me Heaven
> You will surely find her there,

With the angels and St. Gabriel,
Climbing up the golden stair.

The old lips moved, but no sound came . . . And here was a very special piece of ribbon in the school colors—from the marshal's baton at graduation exercises. Here was the little note that still made her heart flutter: "Miss Mattie Sylvester." Her trembling fingers drew it again from its time-browned envelope, though its message was brief and had been read so often that it was more in her memory than on the page. If its words were banal, she had never been aware of it. To her, they spoke from the heart.

Dear Mattie:
I am sitting here thinking of last night in the moonlight, down on the steamboat wharf. I love you more than life itself. Nothing shall ever part us.
Jim

There were others like it over the ensuing months, lost somewhere in the precious clutter. And here was the longer one, with the picture postcard of Morro Castle enclosed.

Dearest Mattie:
It seems appropriate that the fellows from this town that have signed up in the navy should have been assigned to the battleship "Maine." She is a big and powerful ship of which we can all be proud. At present we are anchored in the beautiful harbor of Havana . . .

There was more—and then those precious words of love repeated (she pressed it briefly to her gray and wizened lips) and, "Mattie, if there should be a child . . . when I return . . ."

Her mind bobbed back again in that unpredictable way it had, perhaps partly because the ghosts of the old house were so much with her tonight. She guessed she really *had* married the house, come to that. The townspeople had been surprised when Cap'n Warren had led to the altar that quiet, prissy little person, already well on the road to spinsterhood. "Miss Mattie!" they said. "Why?" Miss Mattie who, as everybody could tell you, over the long years of her virginity had never had time for the thought of a man! Her husband was not only well to do, but a genuinely good man and a model of devotion. Together they refurbished the house, made it bloom again. She loved the old things—the china, the linens, the silver; she set a perfect table and he was a lavish host.

Her thoughts wandered through the maze that seemed to be their constant haunt: the laughter that filled the rooms, the electric candelabra that reflected softly from silver place settings, the elite of their small community gathered there, flowers from their garden, the Madeira, small-town gossip blending with talk of the sea—the sound of the sea. A dress of marrowy china silk . . . How long ago had it been—fifteen years, ten years, a month, yesterday . . . ? Her head was dizzy and her eyes closed. "And now, Lizzie, the cheese and crackers; and tea (she whispered the aside so none of the guests could hear) in the best Limoges . . ."

Dimly she became aware that the warmth which had bathed her face, her chest, her knees, had withdrawn. Her back was cold. Yes, it was snowing, and she was drawing upon her last ounce of strength to reach the house—her house, that Warren had made beautiful and comfortable for her . . . But no, here she or somebody sat in the leather rocker. She had made it, then! But why the snow, the cold, Ah yes, the fire! There was only gray ash and a few lingering sparks in the depths of the fireplace. It was painful to rout this stiff old body out of its cocoon—but she must restore the life-giving warmth. Several small spruce logs still stood in the capacious copper scuttle—yes, spruce—that was the thing, quick and intense while it burned, though it hadn't the lasting qualities of beech or maple. It sputtered and you had to watch it; she'd need to put up the fire screen, which she hadn't used so far. But the kindling was gone; how to ignite those few glowing coals? Slowly, heavily, yet feeling like some disembodied spirit, she made her way back to the kitchen, automatically dropped a couple more chunks into the King Clarion and checked the draught. Then she picked up the can of kerosene—it held only two gallons and fortunately for her limited strength it was not full. She made her slow progress back to the living room and turned the can upside-down over the coals.

Sam Eaton, coming back in the early morning hours from securing his lobster boat against the gusts that accompanied the blizzard, was first to see the glow against the sky. Of course by the time they hooted the hooter over the town house, the boys got to the village fire house, and Malcolm backed the pumper out into the storm, it was obvious that they could do little. One of the houses out at the end of Sylvester Road, they figured: Sammie Weed or Sylvanus or Ambrose Pickering. But as they bucked the drifts, it became obvious that the glow was farther than that.

They came to a halt where the improved road ended: the tunnel of trees was drifted in too heavily to breach. Sizeable birches and young spruces were weighed down across the road. Miss Mattie's! But who would have taken shelter there on a night like this? It was only in the midst of the smoldering embers on Christmas morning that they found out.

VII

And What Life Is

This story, originally published in *The General Magazine and Historical Chronicle* (1954; LVII, Nos. 1 and 2, pp. 31-36), is based on an actual incident. The main character, Frank Weed, ran a store selling groceries and dry goods, according to Chatto and Turner's *1910 Register*. The building is still there, at the intersection of Route 15 and the Lowe Road. For a time around 1950, it saw service as an ice-cream shop run by Frank's granddaughter, Hazel Torrey, but mostly since Frank's time it has been a private residence.

Although Tom used made-up names for all the characters, we have changed them back to the originals. Even so, some of the ancillary characters are fictional, and there has been some scrambling of generations. Whatever "yowuns" were involved in the search, they were not George C's, as they had not yet been born.

One term that modern readers may find puzzling is the "tonic" consumed by the searchers. Time was when "tonic" was the generic term for any carbonated beverage, from Moxie to Coca-Cola. The term was still in use until after World War II.

☙ And What Life Is ❧

Frank Weed pulled up the dappled mare just short of his big barn door. His grey eyes roved approvingly over fields that reached far back to the spruce woods, a habit of well-nigh onto forty years. Unconsciously his shoulders squared slightly, still broad for all time's passing and the sand in the hair above them. Not an alder, not a nubbin of granite marred his view, and off in the swamp acre above the crisscrossing ditches his pickaxe had wrested from the clay and hard-pan, a second crop of hay was waving thick and ready for the mower. Folks had called it a mad idea, that swamp acre, and said he'd kill himself, the hours he worked. He'd have it a lot easier, they said, yachtin' over to Bar Harbor or Northeast; that's where the money was now. Well, he'd never been afraid of work.

Was he wrong in his thinking a large part of the trouble was, nowadays, that hardly a soul on the island got up for five a.m. breakfast—to put the cows to pasture, feed the hens and collect the eggs, or to make up a batch of yeast bread for the week, and get the washing out? Come to that, they wa'n't any cows, hardly, or hens neither. Folks was content to buy their milk in bottles from over to Bangor or Ellsworth way—and three quarters of the cream skimmed offen it. By King! He'd never expected to see the day. What with the price of feed, they said it was cheaper to buy eggs than to raise them. Last case he'd had in the store come clean from Canada, it did. And the women-folk washing by machine! Ayuh, a lazy world and the old stock petered out. Firs and junipers taking over the pasture lots and crowding in from the stone walls round the plowed land. Folks seemed to have forgot what a brush-hook was for. Not many fields like his!

The mare flirted her check rein and lifted one foot gently to dislodge a fly, but she was used to standing. Frank sent an affectionate glance over her glossy back. The grocery cart had done well on the road that morning; they'd got nigh on to Carman's Rock. Why should he plague himself if all the housewives along the Deer Isle Road preferred to buy bakery bread in wax paper packages? Just that much more trade for him. Maybe he should have him one of them little Ford panel jobs b'um'bye; he cal'lated he could get as far as the summer colony at Dunham's Point then. But, King! The rusticators had their Buicks and their station wagons; they got up to the store for his homemade ice cream smart enough. Liked it, they did, and kept him churnin' plenty ahead. The heft of their trade went to the stores in the village. Cap'n Annis, with his big Bangor produce truck—Flying Yankee, he called himself—liked to mock him about the horse. "Frank," he said, "them critters is as much out of style as a gaff-rigged sloop. If Noah had the job to do over, he'd take a tractor aboard the Ark." But King-darn-it, he was fond of the dappled mare; he'd sat up half the night while the old horse foaled—and Eliza to keep him company, stoking wood into the cook stove to keep the kettle hot and a pot of coffee boiling. Eliza . . .

The marble stone in the cemetery over to the Haulover had been there a week now. Handsome thing, it was, with the carving at the top. Cypress trees seemed a bit out of place in the state of Maine, but when he'd told what he had in mind, the man from Fletcher and Butterfield had said they was a symbol of sorrow. And there must be an urn carved beneath them—to hold his tears, he guessed: ELIZA, BELOVED WIFE OF FRANK WEED, 1857–1918. And in nice block letters the text:

SHE DONE WHAT SHE COULD.

Fig. VII-1. The gravestone of Frank Weed and his wife (at Mount Adams, not the Haulover) differs from Tom's description. It does, however, bear the inscription "She done what she could" in small letters at the base of the stone. Photo by William A. Haviland.

Fig. VII-2. This is the building as it looked in 2002 that once housed Frank Weed's store. Photo by William A. Haviland.

They'd writ to ask him about the text; wa'n't somethin' left out? He guessed he knew his Bible, and that's what he wanted: "She done what she could." A right smart woman, Eliza! She'd tended store while he was on the road, and she'd lugged in the wood, as a state of Maine woman should. She'd filled the cellar shelves against the winter with her canning, and she'd kept her kitchen bright. Precious few meetings of the Rockbound Rebekahs or the Star she'd missed, never mind the weather. Come sickness or come trouble in town, she was there to do her part. Ayuh. And never a spleeny moment.

There hadn't been much time for foolishness after he first brought her into the neat little white-clapboard farmhouse he'd had a hand in the buildin' of, with its massive central chimney. Mostly they was tired, nights—stayed home and tended to lanchin' a family, as folks should. A time at the Grange together, an occasional night trompin' down the Lady of the Lake and the Portland fancy at the town house, a new dress now and then from Sears' big catalogue, Labor Day at Blue Hill Fair—and then, of a sudden it was their twentieth anniversary. They took the boat to Boston over the weekend. By King! It was a new world: the trolley cars, the Common, South Church, Bunker Hill, the vaudeville. But cities are ugly, noisy places. Glad to get back to the island again, they was—to the store and the farm and the children. After they'd got the boy off to sea like their grandfathers before them and the wee ones were woman grown, there'd be time for play. They'd slack off a mite then. He'd started to rib up a boat after they got back—Eliza dearly loved the water. Its frame stood now, a gaunt skeleton, in one corner of the barn. Well, come to think on it, perhaps those years of work together had been really play . . . Might be the two were one.

Took the spice out of life, her being called; didn't seem much sense to it from here on. Of course they was still the girls. Annie and Esther were married and living their own lives, but Kate and Helen were still to home—Kate a tall girl but otherwise the spittin' image of her comfortably made mother, too much so, perhaps. Folks still minded the time she recited "The Wreck of the Hesperus" at graduation from the high school. But somehow it gave him a turn. And at the dances she was a dazzling, wild thing. He lifted his eyes meditatively out past the corner of his barn to the deep autumn blue of Sprucehead and the Camden Hills; maybe, as some off islanders said, families were too mixed up for their own good—too many Haskells married to Haskells, too many Eatons married to Eatons . . . too many Weeds married to Weeds.

The trouble hadn't come on Eliza till these last few years, though, and then so slow a body hardly noticed it first off. She got forgetful; then after a spell her mind would go blank-like, every so often, and she'd wander off in a fog. King! She'd failed, too, these last five years. Sometimes he and the girls would have to turn out after her, to find her sitting wide-eyed in some angle of the pasture wall. Next day, like as not, she'd be right as a dollar again.

It was Frank Milan, stuffing the R.F.D. boxes at the top of Hardy's Hill with Monkey Ward's *Fall and Winter Catalogue* that hailed his cart with the news Eliza had disappeared, and the girls were well nigh distracted.

Fig. VII-3. The home of Howard Lowe, one of the searchers for Eliza Weed, as it looks today. It once was the parsonage for the North Deer Isle Congregational Church. Photo by William A. Haviland.

Soon's he met Kate on the store piazza, he saw how things stood. Well, they was just one way to sign a crew on in a hurry. He cranked one long and three short on the store phone. As he listened he could hear the click of receivers in anticipation of some choice morsel. His alert ears picked up the muffled bark of Grace's rat terrier and the gentle rhythmic cheep of the latest batch of chicks—it didn't seem to matter what the season—by Doris' kitchen stove. The womenfolk were never too far from the phone. And Bessie Torrey was said by all to be the most constant source of gossip on the four-two line. "If only," Eliza often said, "the fat thing wouldn't burp right into the phone!" Eliza swore someday she'd say right out loud: "Excuse me." She'd teach the woman some manners! Frank waited until he was sure his audience was assembled. "Eliza's cruised off somewhere," he announced. "We'd be beholden if them as could would give us a hand."

George C's yowuns were first, and one took the word up to his father, who was peeling pulp with Hector the French Canadian back among the big spruces in the Rocky Hills. Then came the older folk as lived handy—Howard Lowe, Amos and Ida Margaret with some of the girls, Ebenezer and Moodie Powers, and Isophenie, and, before the afternoon was over, the crowd that were still raking blueberries for the factory in Emily's pasture. They scattered into groups of two or three—out into the Torrey field, down Garfield's lane to the mouth of the Trout Stream, over the wood road to the lonely, fire-charred cellar of the Dexter Place, and so to the lime quarry and the deep, forbidding asbestos pit. As the afternoon wore on, it became clear that they'd find her in none of the likely places. It was uncommon hot and dry. Joe Pye Weed had shed its handsome pink, the michaelmas daisies were beginning to brown up already, and only a faint breath from the sou'west came in across the bay. The weather, Frank had to admit, in the midst of his growing fears, was good for business, ayuh. Hot and tired, the searchers fished endless bottles of "tonic" from the cooler or bought them a dish of homemade grapenut ice cream, accompanied by a glass of clear cold water from the pump.

As evening fell and a fog-mull settled over Eagle Island, they took to lanterns and bug-lights. Fitfully the sound of the fog bell drifted in across the water. No one—he least of all—would voice what must be obvious to them all: a frightened, bewildered woman of Eliza's years might not survive the night. Hot as it was at midday, the fog was cold and dank, and the wind showed signs of coming round into the northeast. Already he could hear the slow, uneasy roll of the surf on the shore.

By ten next forenoon the fog had burned off, leaving things again damp and humid; the spider webs upon the grass were set with a mass of jewels. The promised breeze had not materialized. He'd ranged as far as the Congo Church by then, after a sleepless night. Some newcomers had joined the search, Charlie Hall among them. Charlie'd left his string of lobster pots to shift for themselves—and a right smart day for hauling, too—

03 03

Frank leaned over the dashboard and contemplated the mare's ears, a wry smile touching the corners of his generous mouth. Good old Charlie. Frank minded the time the Adventists had that mass baptism out Sand Beach way—how Charlie vowed he'd have a ringside seat and anchored his powerboat just about twenty feet offshore. The wind bein' sou'west, she tailed right into the beach. Charlie put two old overstuffed chairs that had been retired to his fish-house onto her stern, and he and Frank sat there watching the Godly being dipped. Quite a crowd of them, they was, and comical enough. When it come Polly Powell's turn, Charlie'd leaned over with a look of anguish on his face. "By Godfrey Damon!" he said, "I'm some glad I give the bottom of this craft a coat of copper paint just yestiddy. If Polly's sins had floated by 'thout it, they'd have corroded every nail in her bottom." How angry Eliza'd been when she heard tell of it: "Making game of all them earnest people. They're Christian folk, even if they do get worked up a mite more than seems proper to you and me." Poor Eliza—

By late afternoon it became pretty clear that what they were searching for was without life. Anxiety gave way to a grim acceptance of the inevitable. Their concern didn't hinder George C's boys from divin' into the ice cream like a school of porpoises (he wondered sometimes how a pulp-wooders yowuns got so much money to spend for sweets) or slack the thirst of Charlie and Francis, big men both, who sweated enough to float a Gloucester dory. They wa'n't so much for the sweet stuff—stuck to cold water mostly.

It was after his third trip to the pump that Charlie Hall made an unhappy suggestion. By King, it was mighty strange they hadn't give it a thought before! Together the three of them went out by the kitchen door and raised the hinged lid. What with the swamp acre no distance off, water was plentiful. There was them that made all manner of fun of a dowsing-rod, but in the spot where his crotched alder pointed to the ground he'd not had to go far down to find a boiling spring. Leaning

Fig. VII-4. The Second Congregational Church (now Episcopal) in North Deer Isle.

high over the well curb now, they a saw a bit of white material dimly. By Godfrey, it gave Frank quite a turn, it did. And possibly some of the thirsty ones, he reflected grimly—

The dappled mare was still content to stand. As Frank's eyes and thoughts roamed back, it came to him all in a rush how tired she looked, the wee colt that Eliza and he had fought for against the night, twenty years gone. Horses and humans—life and death were most often beyond a man's control. You went when your time came. King-darn-it! Life would be a pretty lonely proposition with the partner of nigh onto forty years lying down to the Haulover. But they was still the girls. He'd seen them down the ways, but somehow no likely young fellow had come athwart to their hawse as yet. Didn't seem possible little Kate was gettin' nigh onto thirty!

He clucked to the little mare and gave the reins a flick. Obediently, she tugged at the cart, with its deck-load of groceries and notions, its brooms lashed along the port side, pulling it up the apron into the sweet-smelling gloom of the barn as she had done these many years. That off hind foot was a mite stiff; she'd favored it of late. Frank sighed; well, he thought, as he let himself down over the wheel, he wa'n't so spry himself as once. She'd profit by a spell out with the cows behind the pasture bars. Ayuh. And he?— Well, could be, with the girls to provide for and the friends he'd made on the road over the years, he owed it to himself to drop down to the Granite Garage and just have a look at one of them light trucks.

VIII

'Gustus

Another unpublished piece, this one a nonfiction essay. We are not certain of the real identity of "'Gustus," but a note on one of the cards that Tom used to keep track of characters reads "'Gustus Knight (Warren)." This seems to us to indicate Warren Powers, who lived in a house built by pioneer William Eaton (through whose daughter Warren was a great-grandson). His occupation is listed in the *1910 Register* as "farmer, yachting," and his house lies on a direct route between that of Charles White and the shore. After his death in 1925 (at age fifty-nine) the house was occupied by his daughter and her husband, Garfield Billings, who ran a small dairy farm. The property is still in the hands of their descendants.

The other characters whose identity we are certain of are Charlie White and Tom Haviland himself (see the book's introduction for more on their relationship) and Chauncey (see "Leave by the Lower Deck, Forward"). "Nelse" is Joel Powers, who was indeed a Civil War veteran; he lived in a house on North Deer Isle Road, not far north of the schoolhouse, where the Reach Road begins. The house still exists, but was moved to the shore part of the property in the early 2000s and added onto.

The floundering that Tom mentions would have taken place in the Bowcat, the body of water bounded by Carney Island, the facing west shore of Deer Isle, and the southern end of Little Deer. Before the causeway was built (in the 1930s), this was one of the best places around for flounder fishing. Tom fished with a hand line, but others would spear them. According to Capt. Walter E. Scott (see introduction to "He Maketh the Storm a Calm"), it was not unusual for one boat to spear a barrel of flounders on one tide.

ଓଃ 'Gustus ଓଃ

I

I must have been about nine when I first met 'Gustus, my second summer at Deer Isle. In the garden patch adjoining my cousin's cottage, a stubby figure partly hidden in the rows of beans and corn was grubbing away with infinite slowness and reluctance. "Gussie Knight," my cousin said, nodding at the slow-moving figure—"retired from the sea to spend his declining years on the family farm. Sometimes he hires out to work for other folks if he likes them. Best natured fellow you'd want to meet, but a dubious bargain if you're paying him by the hour."

At this point, having seen us in turn, the figure slowly—oh, so very slowly—pulled itself erect, wiped its forehead and addressed my cousin in an expressionless drawl which I find even now difficult to characterize in print: "Saay, Chaarliee . . ."

"Yes, Gussie."

"You got a hoe over theree . . . ?"

"Sure. You want to borrow it?"

Fig. VIII-1. Charles White's house. It still stands today, at the end of "Louise Haskell Way."

The figure ruminated for almost a whole minute. Then the same slow, expressionless drawl: "Yees . . . fetch it over, will ye?"

My cousin lowered his voice for my especial benefit. "Laziest man in God's great world."

II

Our second meeting occurred when I must have been eleven. Usually, my father or my cousin went flounder fishing with me, but on this occasion I had been trusted to pull the skiff down over the pebbly beach alone. The Bay was calm, the tide right, and my luck reasonably good. Certainly no more than a couple of hours had elapsed in a boy's long day before I had beached the skiff again well up the shore on a coming tide and made her fast to a tree. Rather than take the winding town road, I found it much more convenient to cut up across 'Gustus' pasture (I use the term in the broadest sense, for it consisted largely of little isolated grassy oases in the midst of a flourishing growth of alders, poplars and hackmatacks. The two Guernseys did what they could, but each year, as the trees and bushes crowded in from their margins, the little oases grew smaller. 'Gustus allowed that someday he'd have to take a brush-hook to the intruding growth, but somehow he never got to it.

I found him to the south of the hummocky lane that led up between his house and barns, sitting in the sun on his chopping block, in the pleasant lee of the old yellow carriage house. He greeted my approach with what seemed his usual enthusiasm—that inflectionless drawl: "Hii, you." He spat out a great chaw of tobacco. Indications were that he had recently been "manufacturing" two-foot chunks of spruce into kindling for the kitchen stove—but not too many. "What you got there?" he drawled.

"Flounders," I said, displaying my string proudly.

"Flounders!" He contrived to invest the word with the ultimate degree of disgust, "I'd as soon eat skunk as flounders!— Here, let me trim 'em up for ye." He laid them one by one on the block and with leisurely, well-aimed blows of the axe, snipped off head, tail and fins, which he scraped to the ground to gather flies and yellow-jackets for the next couple of weeks.

Decent appreciation seemed to demand that I tarry awhile on an adjoining upended keg, during which time the expressionless face digested without sign and silently filed away the result of his catechizing as to where I lived in the wintertime, what my father did, how much my

Fig. VIII-2. Tom's cousin Charlie White and his dog Bob.

father made, just how we were kin to the Whites, what grade I was in at school— As my answers seemed to call for no comment, our conversation languished. I presumed to put a question of my own, on a matter that had bothered me on several previous trips through his barnyard.

"'Gustus," I said with the temerity of youth, "you're going to think I'm plenty nosey. My cousin was talking the other night about something he couldn't figure out. He said you like to do things the easy way, but this woodpile, now, is clean on the other side of the lane from your kitchen door."

His attention thus directed, he scrutinized as though it were something totally new, the heterogeneous pile of sawed stove-lengths that lay beside us. "Ayuh," he offered—partly as confirmation, partly as encouragement to proceed to my point.

"Well, look," I said, "there's nothing in your back dooryard but a crop of burdocks and a few old broken wagon wheels. What's to prevent your dumping the load there? That way, your wife wouldn't have to lug it so far a couple times a day. She could just pop out, gather up an armload of sticks, and pop right in again."

He regarded me fixedly, not without a faint hint of disapproval. He retired within himself to meditate, then came up with the answer which I'm sure he felt should have been perfectly obvious, even to a young fool like me. "That woodpile . . . ? Why do I have it theree . . . ? Weell . . . my father had it there, and my grandfather had it there, and I cal'late that's why I have it there."

"Yes," my cousin said later, "'Gustus is what you might call a traditionalist."

III

It was election day. Just ahead of us, 'Gustus in his old two-seated wagon was drawn up before Captain Ky's. On the rear seat sat Nelse, wry-backed, with his great gray beard and piercing eyes. A Civil War veteran, he had become permanently bent when a tree fell on his back, so that he hobbled now with a cane. It would have killed a lesser man. Whether as a result of the accident I never knew, he was not quite right. He suffered a persecution complex and ranted that the boys from Little Deer came in their peapods, crept up from the shore, and stole his plums, his pears, his catnip, and various exotic herbs from the small garden on which he lavished tender care, down behind the white house and barn. One day, as I had rounded a turn in the road quite alone, I first came face to face with the awesome figure, shuffling along with his cane. Before I could move prudently to the other side, he seized me by the shirt-front, fixed that steely gray eye upon me, and starting at no logical taking-off place, roared: "I say Norway maple is the only kind a man should trust. You take them silver maples, now—they're punky inside. The gophers get in them, and the foxes get into them, the wolves eat them—" I died a thousand deaths till the fierce old eyes suddenly softened; he released his grasp, and I was free to scuttle past.

Yes, Nelse was not quite right! He and Cap'n Ky and 'Gustus were brothers. As we drew abreast of 'Gustus' rig, my friend made an inclusive gesture with his whip—Ky, Nelse and himself—and announced in the familiar drawl, "All the crazy Knights going down to the Town House to vote Democratic." The town was Republican.

"A strong party man," my cousin observed, "and though in this case he may not completely exaggerate his family's state, something of a humorist."

IV

Chauncey and I had overtaken our septuagenarian friend on the three-and-a-half-mile hike from the village. It was August, and in the light of a good-sized moon, the locusts were talking shrilly. The dirt road was hard, dry, and dusty. "Now slow down a mite, lads," Gussie counseled, "and keep a body company. There's nowhere to go but bed." And so, as he plodded steadily, solidly along, that drawl, capable of taking on humorous overtones, turned to experiences at sea—and then settled on a somewhat lengthy report of his sexual prowess, which had known no barriers of race or color during those distant days in foreign ports. Having run with the country boys, I was far better acquainted with the facts of life than my city-bred contemporaries back home or than my somewhat Victorian parents were aware, but I heard things that night, with no details omitted, that opened both my ears and eyes. His monologue required no comment from his two intent listeners, to whom he paid the high compliment of experiences shared between men.

As we stopped before his comfortable story-and-a-half farmhouse, the lovely sweep of its roof unmarred by dormers, he terminated the lengthy recital. "You know my daughter May?" he inquired of me, with a dying fall. And before I could answer yes or no, "Think you could hold her down?" At fourteen I was still shy of girls, so I could not be sure whether this was a purely academic question—or a sort of invitation. Ultimately, I discovered it was a mere parental pleasantry that he put to others besides me. In due time, May, who to my knowledge was a thoroughly proper young lady, as island girls went, did find over in Rockland one who could and would—and did.

"Horny old bastard," Chauncey said, as we walked off into the night.

V

There was good pay over at Mount Desert those days in the summer months, for one who would go captain and crew of one of the numerous little sailing craft that raced out of Bar Harbor and Northeast or dotted the waters of Somes' Sound. "By Godfrey, you," 'Gustus said, "never had no experience outside of schooners, but I've done a heap of sailin' in my time. Come to think of it, I'm kind of rottin' away on shore; I'll give it a try."

Nobody could miss the fact that 'Gustus was a saltwater man. It got him a job right off on a trim little thirty-footer. The owner became quite fond of him and his picturesque vocabulary; he swallowed without question some of his new captain's tall stories about his early days on coasting schooners. In general, though 'Gustus might be a bit shy with the mop, the scrubbing brush and the brass polish, he could con a sail in a breeze as well as most. In the biweekly races, however, the owner sailed the *Seagull* himself, and Gussie's station, not at all disagreeable to him, was up bow, where he leaned back against the stays, one firmly gripped in his big red fist, and kept watch for hazards to navigation.

A fair wind out of the nor'west had broken the flat calm of the September morning, raising dancing little whitecaps on Frenchman's

Bay. *Seagull* was taking the long reach before the wind for the second yellow keg that marked the course of the final regatta of the season. With a bone in her teeth, she was fairly flying. The owner had jockeyed her across the line just right as the gun went off and was showing her pursuers a clean pair of heels. 'Gustus stood swaying with the motion as she dipped and raised her prow gently to the rhythm of the seas.

Suddenly, insofar as this was possible, the expressionless drawl of the watch in the shrouds contrived a note of urgency, "Haard over! Haard over!" The course was laid out free of obstacles, but there was always the danger to a light-planked boat of a floating tree or a heavy piece of timber. The owner brought her abruptly into the wind; the sail slatted idly, and she lost way. In the few precious seconds, two of their nearest competitors sailed by to starboard; he took a turn around the tiller and a few steps forward. "God, 'Gustus, what's the matter—a log?"

"Matter?" the slow voice echoed provokingly. "No matter; just goin' too fast, I cal'late."

The following season, Gussie's job was filled by a man from Swan's Island.

"Well," my cousin said, "his voice doesn't come out that way for nothing. He's just not geared for speed."

VI

The light buggy eased over the crest of the Southeast Hills, and all the dapple-gray had to do was hold back in the traces and keep the rig from rolling over her heels. We had covered half the distance to Stonington, a real adventure, for the jaunt was a good fourteen miles, and all the previous day the horse had been rested in preparation. 'Gustus had heard about a man who wanted to sell his boat, he told me; he aimed to look her over. We had jogged easily down the narrow dirt road, through the village, past small marginal farms nestled among the spruce trees, enjoying vistas of the Bay, and dropping down past the small, sandy coves that sharply indented the land.

'Gustus was in rare spirits, and since I was sixteen now, he apparently felt no further responsibility for acquainting me with the facts of life. Other than a sly poke in the ribs and the flattering question as to whether I was "getting much these days," he concerned himself with names and thumbnail sketches of the folk who inhabited these very distant and foreign parts. He seemed unusually well informed. The man we were seeking out was named Pearl Stinson. So when, in due course, the ribbon of road led us to a large gray house by the water, and 'Gustus drove through the dooryard and into the beautifully kept red barn, though there had been no name on the R.F.D. box, I began speculating which of the boats lying offshore was Pearl's. In leisurely fashion 'Gustus unhooked the check rein, removed the bit from the mare's mouth, pulled down some hay from the mow, and casting about to find a measure, filled it partly with oats and set it on a keg for her. Then we left by the side-open doors.

A man stood on the side piazza of the house, looking at us inquiringly. 'Gustus greeted him with his friendliest grin: "Say, mister," always that toneless drawl, "don't know what your name is. I put my horse in your barn. You don't mind, do you?"

So it wasn't Pearl Stinson's, then? We were to discover that Pearl lived some quarter mile around the shore. 'Gustus stood there, that infectious grin undiminished; he couldn't have been less perturbed.

"Mind?" said the figure on the piazza, and though it was sarcastically begun, his reply warmed in mid-career, "no, take the house, too. It's yours—"

"Yes," my cousin said when I recounted my adventure that evening, "Gussie has a way with people."

VII

Having once had his taste of the sea again. 'Gustus was not to be denied. He finally bought an old hulk with a winch for hauling, rammed the cotton caulking into her wide-open seams, and painted her a bright green. Then he built him some wooden traps and set up in the business, but he was an indifferent lobsterman at best. It was not his age; there were two out of Stonington who still fished solo at eighty-five.

The old Buick conversion job was thoroughly undependable, and 'Gustus possessed absolutely no feeling for machinery. His gear, too, was always in a mess. Pots became fouled on the bottom of the bay, or the killicks were insecurely wedged into the slatted floor, so that the cussed things came up and floated. And his cockpit was a litter of old bait pockets, fouled and knotted pot warp, an anchor and its hopelessly tangled rope that should have been up bow. When he hauled a trap, throttling her down, setting his rudder to circle the spot, he never bothered to feed the incoming line into a coil as it came off the drum.

"Can't figger, it, nohow," his fellows said. "'Tain't the way his father brung him up on the schooner. Why, he'd a whaled hell out of the boy.

Wonder Gussie lasted a week with that feller over to No'theast. Just gone plum lazy," they said, "and headed for trouble. Gawd, you wait and see." How right they were.

When Vergil Weed spied the familiar green boat circling meaninglessly off Great Spoon Island he already knew the answer. Coming alongside, he climbed aboard amidst the clutter and cut the power. No traces of 'Gustus; there was no line on the drum outboard. Vergil dropped a buoy at the spot, made the boat fast to his stern and headed home, scanning the shore of Great Spoon as he went by, just in case. The lobster fishermen kept an eye out, particularly on the third day, but it wasn't till the fifth that the body rose, the pot-warp still wrapped around one leg.

"Well," folks said, "never was in a hurry, that Gussie Knight. He'd take his time, you can depend upon it!"

IX

Cap'n Cecil and the Littlest Steamboat

Another character portrait, but in this case we know the true identity of its subject. In reality, Cap'n Cecil is Arthur Campbell, who Chatto and Turner's *1910 Register* lists as a farmer and lobster buyer. He was the great grandson of John Campbell, who came from Argyllshire in Scotland around 1780 and acquired close to five hundred acres of land on the Reach. Arthur's mother, Diana Carr (Hardy) Campbell, was herself a granddaughter of John Campbell's daughter. A bachelor all his life, Arthur lived in the old Campbell homestead at Poplar Point. (It had fallen into disrepair late in the twentieth century, when the Deer Isle Fire Department demolished it as a means of practicing firefighting.)

Arthur's wharf was located at the old homestead, and its remains can still be seen. To take live lobsters to the steamboat wharf at Stonington, he took advantage of the high water to take the shortest route: across the sandbar that connected Sunshine with Mountainville. The present causeway was not built until 1935; the causeway mentioned in the story was not the modern one but the so-called Indian Causeway mentioned in "Days of the Buckboard." This actually was not a causeway at all but an ancient Indian fish trap that ran along the sand bar. Exposed from half to low tide, shallow-draft boats could easily pass over it on the flood.

Arthur's boat, here named the *Grace and Alice*, was actually the *Swastika*, but this was before the rise of Nazi Germany. The emblem had not yet become the symbol of evil that it later did.

Tom's geography gets a bit creative in this piece. The Drunkard is

ଓଃ Cap'n Cecil and the Littlest Steamboat ଓ

Cecil Mac Corrison pushed the stiff straw hat, battered and browned, that he wore summer and winter alike, onto the back of his head and wiped the sweat off his brow. He'd just rolled the last of twenty barrels packed with lobsters up to the head of the slip at the steamboat wharf in Stonington and was back in the cockpit readying up. The heat rising from the upright boiler in the little *Grace and Alice* added to the discomfort of the August day. Its asbestos coating was pitted with rusty holes, the brass-work was green with verdigris, and the valves and pipe joints gave off whiffs of steam.

Tall and spare, he wore an old pair of gray wool trousers and a flannel shirt which had faded to a nondescript bronzy pink. He cast a meditative eye over the half-dozen other craft chafing gently against the pilings. Ben Staples, pausing from sluicing down the decks of his trim lobster boat

Fig. IX-1. All that remains today of "Cap'n Cece"'s house (the Campbell homestead) is its foundation, still impressive in its size and construction. Photo by William A. Haviland.

Fig. IX-2. The littlest steamboat: the *Swastika* at Campbell's Wharf.

with her new Mianus engine, had just asked the inevitable question (they liked to plague him with it): "Cece, why'nt you get rid of that old peanut roaster clutterin' up half your cockpit and put in a good gasoline engine? A fellow's got to keep up with the times. You leave steamboatin' to the Eastern and the Maine Central. Get a little speed into her, too. You take and paint out your hull and decks and you'd have a right slick little craft."

His answer had become a set part of the ritual: "Sh-she ain't as handsome as your bu-boat, mebbe. And she ain't so fast. Bu-but, King-darn-it, she's got p-p-power!"

Just short of thirty feet, the *Grace and Alice* was undoubtedly the smallest steamboat on the bay—solid-timbered and a workboat through and through. Beside the towering white *Pemaquid*, she was ridiculous, but she had never been accused of being a thing of beauty, even in her halcyon days. Now her paint was grimy, and the curtains that pulled down around her standing room to form a foul-weather shelter were frayed and torn. But religiously she chose her time right, plodded her way up the Eastern Bay and waited for the coming tide to flood the sandy causeway—between Sunshine and Mountainville. Then, shallow draft as she was, she eased her way across with her barrels of lobsters netted in Cece's pound, to land the precious cargo on the steamboat wharf for transshipment to Rockland and Boston. From the bottomless gallon paint can that served as her funnel, to the rust-pitted coating of her boiler, she was the personification of poverty.

Fig. IX-3. Campbell's wharf as it appears in 2002. Photo by William A. Haviland.

It wasn't that Cap'n Cecil was poor, himself, Godfrey no! He'd made a small fortune from his lobsters and from the hay he cut in the broad meadow he'd cleared and drained into a big pond at its center. The barn he'd built to hold the hay was monstrous. No, as befitted his Scotch ancestry, he was merely frugal, and, being a bachelor, a mite queer, folks allowed; when a man lives alone without womankind, he'll take to doing peculiar things. There was the time Cecil heaped all the pods, from the peas he'd shucked out for meals, in a corner of the kitchen by the old iron sink two years a'runnin'. And the spell when he'd painstakingly piled his burnt matches crisscross into a tower at the end of the big wood-burning King Kineo. Winters he went to Florida.

But his mates liked to think he was snug. "The old skinflint," they'd say, running a disapproving eye over the dripping joints and the little jets rising here and there from the pipes on the *Grace and Alice's* boiler. "Way 'tis, one of these days that old boiler's going to let go." They'd see him on a straightaway course up the Reach, loop a piece of line over the wheel, amble in his loose-jointed stride down stern, reach a couple two-foot lengths from the pile he kept there and stoke them into his boiler. When Ben Staples passed him down by The Drunkard Ledge, on the same course forenoons, his make-and-break engine putting smoothly, the routine was always the same: "Hi Cece, whyn't ye get a gasoline engine in that slow-freight?" Cecil'd grin as they pulled apart: "I cal-late these here l-lobsters ain't in no p'pa'ticular hurry." He yanked the cord and produced a shrill blast on his little whistle. Ben chuckled, "I never see one of them peanut roasters up to the city," he observed to himself, "but it must sound just like that."

In or out of port, the *Grace and Alice* and her master were fair game, but nothing the boys ever did seemed to rile Cap'n Cecil. Like the day when, after they'd trucked their barrels up the slip, a humorist from Stonington suggested, "A fellow ought to carry a nightshirt aboard, the rate that craft o'yourn moves." It gave Ben a wonderful idea. While the agent heated up the pot of coffee for Cecil, on top of the little pot-bellied stove in the place boarded off from the freight house for an office, Ben and a half-dozen others in the crowd raided the Widow Dow's clothes line for a red flannel nightgown. (There was always some devilment afoot at the steamboat wharf!) They hauled it to the top of the little pole aft that Cece had rigged his stern light on, managed to jam the line in the pulley, then cut it just beyond a tall man's reach.

Cece, as usual, took it in his stride. The cavernous blue eyes astride his aquiline nose glowed humorously. "C-c-cal'late *Grace and Alice* needs a f-f-flag down stern. I ain't never had the t-time to rig one up— But could be the widow's goin' to f-f-find it cold-sleepin' tonight, you."

"Whyn't you offer to sleep with 'er, Cece? She'd take a bit of warmin' up, I figger— And besides, that craft o' yourn'll never make it back down the bay 'fore night sets in."

Come mid November, Cecil could have taken a bit of warming up, himself. The better part of the night he'd been hard put to clean out his pound on the low drain by lantern light, to barrel the last of the lobsters on the coming tide and ice them for market. Now, in the chill of early dawn, with the tide flood again, he had to own himself pooched. But at least when the Rockland boat pulled off for the winter he'd have the satisfaction of knowing that the last of his lobsters were aboard. He'd fired the *Grace and Alice's* boiler an hour ago; the steam sang in the glow.

Having come up so high, the tide was ebbing fast; now, as he watched the steady climb of the indicator hand on his gauge, he shook his head; there wouldn't be too much time to spare at the causeway. He chucked a couple more maple chunks into the firebox; the heat from the open door felt grateful. He hated to leave it, but he swung up on deck and edged along to the bow to toss the mooring pennant off the cat's-head. It was really brisk; winter was not too far off. Back at the helm, he opened a valve, slowly at first, until he'd given her all the steam she'd take. The propeller thudded and the shaft vibrated in its leg as the little craft took a bone in her teeth and headed into the slight northwest chop, the last rags of the old red nightgown flapping from the pole astern. She was settling down nicely to her job, and Cap'n Cecil, in his small pilothouse backed his chilled bones as close to the old boiler as he dared. He checked anxiously on the tide as he gave the necessary berth to The Drunkard. Somewhere hereabouts he should make his usual rendezvous with Ben. He smiled at the thought of their time-hallowed interchange. He could still take the shorter passage inside, but the rockweed on the boulders at the top was exposed, and the kelp reached long fingers menacingly from below. Directly ahead, a familiar boat drifted, wallowing gently in the swell. As the *Grace and Alice* approached and pulled abeam, Ben Staples crawled out of his cuddy. Cecil's long face was all agrin; this time it was his turn.

Fig. IX-4. The steam engine from the *Swastika*, now in the cellar of the Deer Isle town hall. Photo by William A. Haviland.

"Ben, whyn't yer get ye one of them new g-g-gas engines?"

"Gawd, Cece, the trip spring on my friggin' igniter's pooched, and I ain't got me no spare."

"Ayeh."

"See you're headin' for the *Pemaquid* with your critters, too. You couldn't give a fellow a tow?"

Cecil looked speculatively at the line of eel grass and foam along the shore. "We'd never make it, you! If you ain't g-get her started up 'time I get back, I'll t-t-toss you a line."

Staples' tone was pleading: "Cece, for Gaw's sake don't take it out on me for what I benn sayin' about your boat. I just got to make it somehow. Them six barrels in the cockpit don't look much to you, but with Mae just back from the hospital its all I got in the world. You know they wouldn't keep in the car till spring, Cece."

There was no time for argument. Cecil shut down a couple of valves, put the loose end of a line over a cleat on Ben's deck and lashed them side to side. "It's t-too close figgerin', the way things is, what with that c-c-causeway risin' right up to wait for us ahead. You g-get for'ard and drop an anchor over f-f-fast, then give me a hand with them b-b-b-barrels."

It was heavy lifting as they lay to, and the boiler blew off a puff or two of her precious steam. Then they were plodding off on the last lap, setting low in the water. Grog Island loomed ahead; they had been bucking wind and water, and now the tide rippled and ran fast in the quiet of the lee. Beyond sparkled the narrow expanse of the Reach, its surface dotted with whitecaps. Cap'n Cecil tossed a couple chunks of pasture spruce, rich with resin, into the firebox and slammed the door. The little puffs of steam about the pipe joints grew and the safety valve sounded off.

As they slipped past Grog Island Ledges, Cecil throttled her down a mite. Then both men exclaimed simultaneously. There was a gentle rip over where shortly the breast of the gravel spit would lift out.

"What's she draw, do you figger?" Ben asked.

"'Bout two-and-a-half feet, I cal'late, 'way she's weighted down."

"Gawd, she won't never make it."

Cap'n Cecil tilted his stiff straw hat farther back from off his forehead. "You and your b-b-blasted gasoline engines! If we hadn't lost all that t-t-time down by the D-d-drunkard—"

"Gawd, I'm sorry I held you up, Cece. But if this old hulk could only have stepped a bit—"

"Sh-sh-she ain't never set up to be a sp-speed boat, Ben."

"Well, it's good-bye to my six barrels of lobsters," Ben said. "Heave 'er to."

"D-d-damn your measly six b-b-barrels plumb to hell! 'Case you ain't noticed, I've got close to six hundred dollars tied up in this trip. Take a holt on one o' them stanchions, you."

He opened her up full and drove her for the rip at the center of the sand spit. Ben panicked: "You Gawd-dammed jackass, you'll take the bottom right out'n her!" The water shoaled so fast it looked as if the bottom was rising up to strike them.

She hit with a wallop that brought them up all standing for a moment. There was a jangle and rattle of loose piping; steam jetted from every joint. Ben, despite his handhold, found himself catapulted headfirst amidst three barrels that had broken loose, leaving their ugly occupants crawling dazedly about the cockpit floor, clambering over each other and waving their pegged claws in frustration.

Grace and Alice's upper works seemed to want to keep right on going, while the hull, weighted down by the boiler and her heavy load, was determined to call a halt. Two stanchions cracked, and her paint-can stack fell over the side with a shower of sparks, together with Cecil's straw hat. But in his little pilothouse the skipper kept a death grip on the wheel. She lurched forward another few feet from the sheer impetus, her propeller half out of its element and the sand roiled up for ten feet round. For a breathless moment, she hesitated, her bow reaching out tantalizingly above the deepening water on the far side—then it dropped, and she slid easily down like a skier negotiating a slope.

One of the scrambling cargo had worked a peg loose and had clamped a big claw onto the lobe of Ben's ear. Cap'n Cecil's voice was sharp: "G-G-Godfrey, deah, you get up from playin' with them d-damn c-c-critters. Lift the plank from over the k-k-keelson, you, and stand by with the bilge pump. P-push his damn eyes in; it's the only way to make him let go."

The littlest steamboat seemed to shake herself all over like a dog that had just fetched a stick ashore, then pulled herself together again. Freed of his appendage, Ben looked up from the lifted plank. "She don't seem

Fig. IX-5. The sandbar and "Indian Causeway" between Greenlaw Neck and Sunshine at low tide. When the tide was high, boats like "Cap'n Cecil"'s could pass over the top. Courtesy Deer Isle-Stonington Historical Society.

to've done more'n knocked some of the battin' out along her garboard; don't believe she's really started nothin'." But they were enveloped in a cloud of steam; the pipe from the boiler to the condenser had cracked at an S joint. "My Gawd, she's fell apart," Ben said. "And you just look at the pressure go down. So all-fired near the wharf and now she'll never make it!"

"D-d-don't you worry none about that, old son. J-just you keep an eye on her bilge." Cece ducked under the foredeck and came up with a ragged sheet of asbestos and some fragments of bailing wire. He opened the fire door and checked her, then cast a speculative eye toward the foot of the Reach. He dipped his heavy work gloves over the side and drew them on dripping wet. It was a case of just one more patching job—and he'd done enough already to pass for an expert.

Several layers of asbestos and now several lengths of wire wrapped tightly and swiftly around. Cap'n Cecil snipped the last piece of wire with his rusty pliers, freshened up his fire and opened her drafts wide. She picked up slowly, but again the propeller thudded, the rudder-chain rattled gently in her wake. The steamboat wharf loomed ahead, and a smudge of smoke announced the Rockland boat a couple of miles down the Thorofare. Ben primed the bilge pump over the side and set to; nothing but what he could handle easily, he judged. Doggedly the *Grace and Alice* plodded on the final lap.

Hatless for the first time in years (there were those that said he went to bed in that stiff-rimmed old straw, impossible as it might seem), Cece gave a jubilant blast on his peanut-roaster whistle, then faced astern toward Ben, who was gingerly feeling of his wounded ear. "Why denche g-g-get a gasoline engine in that s-s-slow freight of your'n?" he grinned.

X

Shivaree

The subject of this story is a custom that, like steamboats and dances like the Lady of the Lake, has disappeared from the local scene. But early in the twentieth century it was still customary to have a shivaree on the night directly following a wedding. Though this account is largely fiction, it is an accurate reflection of what went on in these events. It's inspiration was apparently a shivaree for George Armstrong and his wife, who lived in the farm at the end of the Lowe Road.

ങ Shivaree ೪

Dusk had given way to darkness as they made rendezvous at the wood road, then plunged into its dark tunnel. The dozen-odd bore a variety of noise-makers—cow bells, iron "spiders," a lard pail or two with a handful of rocks inside, a conch shell from which its cavorting owner coaxed a series of raucous blasts. They moved quickly up the wheel tracks, avoiding the hummock between, falling into natural groups: the doctor—white-haired, with a face like a ruby—and the young Congregational minister, happy with his first charge; the four teenage boys in the wake of Ida-Margaret's three blonde girls; Young Max and the boy from away; stout Ida-Margaret and Amos—mother and stepfather of the bride—tramping stolidly in the rear. Ahead the big retriever crisscrossed the path, crashing into the undergrowth at intervals in pursuit of some fresh scent.

Since the Morey Farm lay a good two miles ahead, there was no need for caution yet. Rocks clattered experimentally in cans, an iron spoon clashed in march time on a pan. Elroy's harmonica struck up "By the Light of the Silvery Moon," "Merchant's Island," and then "O Dem Golden Slippers," always a prelude to the Lady of the Lake at Odd Fellows Hall. The minister's clear tenor carried the verse of "Merchant's Island" in somewhat expurgated version, better suited to his cloth. There were shouts and laughter from the young folk. Alders and junipers crowded in from the side of the wood road; white birch, fir and spruce rose in a solid curtain behind. Though the late August evening held a tang of the cold to come, the fragrance of the trees, sun-warmed at noon, was all about them.

At the turn, the Hardy Field reached off to the right, silver in the moonlight. With one accord, the shadowy figures rimmed one edge of the road, picking the plump juicy blackberries that clambered right into the alders, staining fingers, lips and teeth purple; some turned their noisemakers temporarily back to their original use as pails to carry along some of the plunder. Perhaps it was the divine contentment of their stomachs that quieted their spirits. The harmonica was muted now, whispering of twilight and love. But the retriever, having raised a snowshoe hare, raced with subdued yelps around the moon-drenched field.

When they resumed their way, scraps of low talk had supplanted their previous hilarity. The doctor and the minister were swapping anecdotes, the old doctor's from his big-city days, so broad in character as to be of no potential value to the minister at a parish tea. Bits drifted back occasionally, "So I walk into the room, and here's a dozen women sitting along the wall and a figure all swathed in blankets and a huge nightcap moaning on the bed . . . You could cut the stench with a knife . . . another damn maternity . . . I single out what looks like the prospective father: 'Go down and get some hot water on,' I order; 'the rest of you clear out!—have that baby in a jiffy'—eyes of my patient all whites!

"'No Doc, don't do that to me! Please, Doc, I'm a man! . . . my reputation in the neighborhood . . . Sure to be thought that if I really put my mind to it . . .'"

The girls chattered like chipping sparrows: "Doris has the cutest new boyfriend . . ." "Remember that little blue dimity in Monkey Ward's catalogue?" "And you won't believe it, but he said to me . . ."

The boys, of sterner stuff, offered deliciously frightened feminine ears talk of bobcats and big snakes underfoot, punctuated occasionally by Elroy's raucous bellow.

Young Max slipped on a loose rock and was thrown against the boy from away. "I've heard tell from my dad," he said, "how, years ago, when folks serenaded old Herbert, who married a girl thirty years younger than him—everybody knew she was a no-account critter—they broke into the house and carried him down-stair in his red underwear. She was bare naked, they said, and hid in the closet. They gave her five minutes to put somethin' on. Then they took down the bedstead and set it up in the front dooryard and lashed the two of 'em in solid. Folks played rough in them days, I guess!— Ain't had a serenade for years. 'Course this one's different; folks like Norman. He's all wool and a yard wide. But sometimes I wonder about this Alida. Can't quite figure why he married up with her."

Amos' spare form, slightly stooped, marched steadily by Ida-Margaret's side, still in the rear of the procession. "Ida-Margaret," his heavy voice was incapable of the whisper he intended, "best call Penny—up there with Elroy. I don't trust him further'n I could heave the port anchor. I seen 'im friggin' round Alida one spell this spring whilst Norman was off to Portland. I was right troubled, I was."

"Now Amos," her own whisper from down in her ample bosom was as coarse as if it came over a nutmeg grater, "you got to just let nature take its course, I say. She's fourteen; time she was thinkin' about gettin' her a man."

"But not that one," he said. "Penny's still just a yowun."

Amos took her plump hand in his as they strode along and ran things through his mind again. Beneath his luxuriant mustache his lips soundlessly phrased his thoughts: Back to the home farm and the sea, still a bachelor at forty and the old man gone. Farm's no good 'thout a woman to share the chores. Never had no truck with women till Sam and Isophenie brought this one around from th' Cranberry Isles. Afeared of the critters for the most part, he was. Hit it off with Ida-Margaret, though, right from the start. Must be what she meant by lettin' nature take its course! But Alida and the other five girls she brought from their foster homes . . . Ayuh, the farm'd got more women that he'd figger'd on! (Kind of vague, too, she was, 'bout where they come from in the first place.) Well, Izora'd got herself a man; now Alida was married to Norman and in due time the others . . .

Slick enough little piece, this Alida, with her long yellow hair and them big blue eyes with the changin' lights in 'em. Pert, too, she was: the things she said, the things she done. Just the way she looked at a body sometimes, through them long silky lashes, or flounced them short skirts and waggled her stern about, did strange things to a man. Did to him anyway! He wouldn't wonder but that . . . Well, he was glad to get her out of the house . . .

From his place in the van, Pete—some said his grandmother Haskell was a full blooded Indian—was the first to spot the glare of headlights in the treetops to their rear and to pick up the roar of the car coming fast, crazy fast for the kind of road it was, little more than a cow path. "Godfrey mighty, it's them! Been to town for refreshments, maybe. Take to the bushes, you!" The retriever with a great arching leap, led the way.

No time to pick a favorable spot in the dark, though there were a couple bug-lights in the crowd. Amos and Ida-Margaret had already crashed heavily into the underbrush; there were laughter and shrill cries. Penny somehow found herself nestled in a bed of sweet fern, still clutching Elroy's hand from the leap. As the Ford careened by, she pressed against him strongly; his hands fumbled with her blouse and found her breasts. She made no move to rebuff him. His breath came hot upon her mouth—

And then with a roar the car was back, and there were voices on the road: "Clamhead, you old son-of-a-sea-cook! Thought 'twas Norm and Alida. Mighta knowed 'twas you, the rate you was a travelin'."

"Gawd no! Heard about the fun, down to the village. Didn't want to miss nothin'. Thought you was all up there by now."

"They see you?"

"Only heard the car. I doused the headlights and put. Light in the cook room. Don't believe they're wise to anything."

Then the hoarse boom of Ida-Margaret's voice: "Penny, you come out of them bushies, or I'll take the hide offen you!"

Clamhead ran the Ford up on an outcropping of granite ledge and left her there while the party covered the last quarter mile. At the driveway into the Weed Farm, they added to their number three more ghostly figures who spoke in tense feminine whispers: "Thought you wasn't never comin'—" "Who was in the car?" "They'll be to bed if we don't hurry."

Everyone was quiet now; even the dog sensed the need. Clamhead joined Max and the boy from away, and the girls blended silently with the lads ahead.

Elroy and Penny walked apart from the rest, hand in hand, in the darkness of the tree-arched road; now and then their thighs brushed. Here was new and untried territory for him. "Penny," he whispered disarmingly, "I don't know how to act. I ain't had no experience with women."

For an answer she squeezed his hand tightly.

And then they were there! A brief moment of reconnoitering. Lights burned in the kitchen, as Clamhead had reported—no lights upstairs as yet. Good! While the doctor deployed his forces, the boy from away found time to admire the fine old white clapboard house with its central chimney. They had been imperceptibly climbing since they left the main highway, and now spread out before him, beyond the house and mowed fields, stretched the far reaches of Penobscot Bay, to his right Eagle Island Light and Owl's Head, blinking infinitesimally small, to his left a broad path of moonlight coldly shimmering and the red flash of Fox Island Thorofare. And above it all, the whole galaxy of the heavens wheeled by in a way to make him dizzy. He became suddenly aware of the high, shrill bowing of a million crickets. He drew in a long, deep breath.

At a signal the tumult broke loose. The conch shell blared raucously, cow bells clanged and pans rattled. The retriever roared hoarsely. A dozen voices cried: "Surprise!" "Norm!" "Alida!" "WE want Norm!" "Open up!"

The kitchen door opened, revealing the bridegroom—tall, slender, his nineteen-year-old face sensitive, his smile flushed.

"Congratulations to the newly-weds!"

"Come in, come in!"

Fig. X-1. The house of "Norman" and "Alida," at the end of the Lowe Road, as it appeared ca. 2006. Photo by William A. Haviland.

The kitchen was warm and fragrant from the crackling spruce wood in the brightly polished Star Kineo. They sat around Quaker-meeting fashion and talked awkwardly for a while, in spite of the young minister's efforts to spark the repartee. And Alida had been fondled by her mother again—and again had given her stepfather that heavy-lidded smile charged with insinuation. Now she passed the refreshments once more—chocolate drops, peanuts, and a pitcher of Kool-Aid, replenished periodically at the pump in the iron sink.

And now, here to greet them was Norman's widowed mother, still a pretty woman, slim, less gauche than the run of farmers' wives, and here miraculously were Ignatius and his fiddle. He plucked a few chords experimentally, made a great show of tightening the pegs, filling his mouth with a swig from his own special bottle each time he tried the strings, till she was tuned just right. They moved back the table and the Hitchcock chairs and the Boston Rocker. At the first tentative bars of "Merchant's Island," the minister offered himself gallantly to Mrs. Morey. Amos dragged Ida-Margaret from the low chair she'd gotten lodged in beneath the painting of the old *Mercantile* under full sail—"Godfrey-Damon, woman, get them fat legs up here!"—and the young folks paired off, Norman and Alida at the head of the set. Norman's brown eyes illuminated his gentle, homely face, as he stood ready with his arm about his new wife's waist.

Alida tapped a trim foot on the art-square, impatient for the music, and flounced her skirt. "Elroy," she called, "you been a settin' on that wood box since you come in the door. You ain't aimin' to spend the whole night like an old gaffer, behind the stove? Ain't you a goin' to dance with me?"

"The next dance is all yours," Norman offered handsomely. Elroy's heavy features flushed, and he brushed an unruly shock of corn-colored hair out of his eyes, "Gawd, I can't," he said. "I ripped out of my pants when we went into them alders back there a piece." *Anyway*, he thought, as the couple balanced down the side, *I already had a little dance with Alida in her father's haymow—and give her somethin' to keep I wouldn't wonder! Hubby may be in for a little surprise come six months or so.*

"Partners balance down the center," Ignatius called, as the fiddle cried and the souvenir dishes rattled in the wall rack.

Penny, slim, girlish in her simple gingham dress, gave Elroy a shy smile as she swung by with Young Max. His close-set eyes followed the action of her hips and thighs.

XI

That Careless Woman

Ambrose, the central character in this piece, is clearly based on Elmer Hardy, one of Tom's neighbors. Born in the house he lived in all his life, he went to sea in 1883 at the age of twenty-two. In the coastwise trade under sail, he later served in the all-Deer Isle crew of the *Defender* in the America's Cup race in 1895. He left the sea shortly thereafter to take over his father's farm, which he worked until his death in 1953.

Although the story line is fictional, various details are accurate: Elmer served on the *Defender*, did sell a piece of hummocky land on the shore to summer folks (Tom's parents); he did blow himself out of the Haviland's well when setting off dynamite; he did begin to build two log cabins to rent out, but never finished them. His son, Luther (the Luke in the story), by 1920 had moved to Brooklyn, New York, where he became a boat and ship builder.

The character Robert Baptiste is based on Arthur Mussells, who had a small store on the main road at the head of what is now called Haviland Lane. He was a French Canadian from Nova Scotia, who did indeed enjoy "chugging about the islands." Evidently he chugged out to Hog Island, near Cape Rosier, with some frequency, for he married the widow of Fred Carver, who ran a farm on Hog Island (see "And Tall Waves Flying").

○₃ That Careless Woman ○₃

Fig. XI-1. Farmhouse in which the real "Ambrose" (Elmer Hardy) and "Lizzie" lived. Built in 1795, it is one of the oldest houses on Deer Isle. Photo by William A. Haviland.

Ambrose had looked with particular eagerness all week to tonight's meeting of Pomona Grange, for the third Thursday of the month meant party night, and there was no denying he loved to dance. For this he put on a clean shirt and his only blue suit, shiny but still serviceable, and slicked down his iron gray hair. His past, his present troubles scaled off like a fog before the sun. He looked covertly at Lizzie, inflexible and slightly grim in her shapeless blue percale topped by the knitted shawl from which she hardly ever parted, silently trudging at his side. The only nights she seemed to care for was when the county agent was there to talk on what to do when your chickens got the pip, or some professor come from the U of M to tell how to feed your pigs to ready them for market faster. Ambrose laughed inwardly: What did these college professors with their book knowledge know that a farmer's own common sense hadn't told him? And of all the silly ideas, hurryin' them porkers. *What's time to a hog?* he thought. Besides, their dilapidated pen hadn't held a pig for years.

Folks agreed that Lizzie wasn't easy to live with. Not that she was spleeny, exactly, but set in her ways. The Howards was like that, and he should have known, but somehow things never worked out for him the way he planned. You take the farm, now. The farm had come to him, its long red carriage house equipped for a lifetime—a big Deering mowing machine nearly new, hay rake, hay kicker and rack, harness lovingly oiled, with a whole mess of forks, shovels, hand rakes, axes, mauls. The large barn, set at right angles, was fully stocked with cattle and sheep. His father had prospered there.

Yes, somehow, in the thirty years he and Lizzie had spent on the old farm bringing up the four boys, things had gone steadily downhill. Seemed like there was a curse on the lot of them. On him, anyway. If he swung an axe, it wasn't long before he sliced his foot; if he mowed a field, the machine brought up on a rock, or the horse got into a yellow jacket's nest, bolted and stove things up. The sheep could never be kept in the pasture, now that the fences were his fences. You'd have said a horse couldn't have got free of his stall and into the feed bin, but the brown gelding had, and foundered himself. The ox was a powerful beast and well trained—but they'd had to butcher him the winter of '16. What blueberries the shore pasture raised, the gulls would take, somehow before he could get around to raking them for the factory.

He looked again at the small figure walking quietly at his side. Well, anyway, she didn't talk a body crazy. By the same token, he supposed, she wasn't one to take up enthusiastically with any new enterprise of his. Like when he'd tried tobacco in place of the quarter acre of telephone peas. "Lizzie, it stands to reason, if they can raise the stuff in Connecticut, we can here. It's just that nobody's tried it; they's money in tobacco." How could he tell peas would bring a record price that year? And the next year he'd tried some tea, but somehow that hadn't made out any better. When he'd got the idea of filling some of the old earthenware milk crocks with yellow-eyes, building a great fire in a pit in the ground and baking them the way he'd heard tell of, in wholesale quantities ("Lizzie, could be we'd start up a whole new industry—and what this island could stand is industry"), all she could think of was to warn him: "Ambrose, them things could build up enough gas to blow you clean to Portland Head. You've done enough foolin' with holes in the ground. You ain't forgot when you was diggin' the well for Mrs. Shuttleworth last year and you set off the dynamite while you was still down there? Wonder it wa'n't the death of ye!"

Yes, Lizzie was a worrisome body. All the winter evenings they set about the house in sweaters and jackets, because she was afeared of fires

Fig. XI-2. The Grange hall, as it looked in 2002. Photo by William A. Haviland.

in the night. If he got a real fire aroarin' in the cookstove, like as not she'd throw a pail of water on it and douse it out. Time was, when they was first married, he'd go to bed with her and warm up—but not any more. If he'd just found him a woman that wa'n't so set in her ways—

Like Lizzie's sister Charlene! When they was both a sight younger, folks thought, 'way he was tendin' out on her, she and Ambrose might have made a match of it. But while he was crewin' on the old *Defender*, Gooden Dow had swept her off her feet. Ambrose'd come back after they'd won the cup, as every crewman had, with good money and a hundred dollar bill as bonus tucked in the sole of his boot—too late. But they was times when he felt Charlene hadn't forgot, not quite.

Nothing but the sound of his and Lizzie's feet on the gravelly road beneath the moon. Though they were early—he had to allow as how he was eager for every moment—Pomona Grange Hall loomed brightly lighted ahead. They were soon going through the mystic ritual with the keeper of the gate, nodded to other early comers and sank down onto one of the hard, straight-backed settles to await the brief formal meeting with which all evenings began. Idly, his eyes took in the titles of the castoff books, mostly from the summer people, that made up the Grange's library: *The Last of the Mohicans*, *The Rise of Silas Lapham*, *Two Years Before the Mast*, *Old Ma'Mselle's Secret*, *Ravished Armenia*, *Mata Hari*.

There was a time, as a young man, when he'd loved to read. On a line with the second shelf sat Charlene—a handsome woman in that bright print dress, even though her hair had silvered and she'd plumped up considerable—flanked by Joyce Pickering and several of the Rockbound Rebekahs.

He was hardly conscious of when the business meeting began, what transpired, or when it ended. But he was in the forefront of those who pushed the long settles back against the walls, while Myra seated herself at the parlor organ, and drums and fiddle took their places.

Before the Portland fancy had more than started, it was his turn to balance Charlene. Folks wouldn't ordinarily allow a parlor organ could step lively at a dance, but they had fun. "See you can still swing a pa'tner right sma't, Ambrose." And "Charlene, you're just as light's ever: It's most as if you was just sailin' in the air like a piece of thistledown." So they had the next waltz together. Lizzie, bein' a strict Baptist, didn't have any truck with dancing. After meetings she'd set with some of the older women from the neighborhood instead and get brought up to date on the latest scandal—for all she wore cotton in her ears winter and summer.

And when the fiddle started up for the next Lady of the Lake, he and Charlene lined up opposite as a matter of course. With Ignatius calling the figures and everybody really in the spirit of the thing, at the cry "Promenade!" the whole lower end went swooping with enthusiastic shouts down the center and through the double doors into the road. Out there under the ancient stars with Charlene's hand warm in his before they swept back into the hall, he could almost have sworn he was a boy again.

The organ wheezed its last note after the strenuous voyage from "Oh Dem Golden Slippers" to "Merchant's Island"; Ignatius lowered his fiddle to mop a red and shining brow; the traps gave a final rattle. And there was Lizzie out in the middle of the floor. "Ambrose, you'd better come along home now."

"King-darn-it! Lizzie, the dancin's not half over."

She looked at him severely: "Ambrose! Puffin' an' pantin' an' carryin' on like a yowun! And you're all of a sweat; you'll catch your death."

"But Lizzie, they's always coffee and pie at the end. We can't leave before that—I'm master hungry."

She took him by the nostrils and towed him out onto the road home. He hadn't missed the snickers as they reached the door—

Fig. XI-3. House of "Cap'n Zeke" (in reality, Lafayette Thompson) as it looks today. Photo by William A. Haviland.

ଔ ଓ

Plodding steadily through next morning's early sunshine toward the turn of the road, Ambrose held the big codfish shrouded in the *Boston Post* at a safe distance from his clean denim shirt and dungarees. Immediately after breakfast—Lizzie started the household functioning promptly at four, even the morning after Grange—he'd cut across the pasture to the shingle beach down by the two cabins for renting to summer folk he'd never finished. His peapod was pulled up in the shade of the alders. The barn chores he'd left to Luke. They wa'n't so heavy a boy couldn't handle 'em easy enough now, he thought wryly—all the result of trying to charge his summer neighbors from the city more than the going price for milk last year. In all the years since he'd sold them the hummocky ground along the shore, they'd been his best customers; they shouldn't have objected to paying a few cents more than other folks.

Prying a few clams loose from under the edge of a rock with his fingers—somehow his clam-hoe had got mislaid—he'd rowed over to the Narrows. The peapod he'd built of some home-cut cedar with Luke's help, sometime back. He had to admit she was a mite rough, and he hadn't the right sort of steam-box to shape the ribs, so that she had a permanent list, which he compensated for with a few chunks of granite on the port side. Of course he had intended to use the boards to patch the back dormer, where the roof leaked more than most places, and Lizzie was some put out— Well, anyway, he'd caught his fish, a fitting present—Charlene hadn't snickered with the rest last night—and with Gooden gone a year, now . . .

He passed Robert Baptiste's little store, not open yet, then the local schoolhouse. He waved to Cap'n Merle on the piazza of his comfortable old house on the hill. Around the turn, Cap'n Zeke's broad red barn, the perfection of nautical neatness, loomed on his left, the double doors wide and the monkey Zeke had brought from South America soberly studying him from the swing to which he was tethered. "God, how the critter stinks!" Ambrose made a face at the memory.

Smoke was rising lazily from the chimney of Elmwood Farm, its clapboards gleaming white in the early sun. How long since his own place had seen a coat of paint! He turned up the path to the kitchen and entered without the ceremony of knocking, island fashion. Charlene, back to the door, was leaning over the freshly blacked cook stove, preoccupied with her preserves. From the rear she presented a well filled expanse not unpleasant to his eyes, topped by a neat gray permanent. Ambrose coughed deferentially.

Fig. XI-4. Lucretia (or Cetti) Closson Staples, the woman on whom "Charlene" is based, lived in this house, built by John Closson (her grandfather) in 1820. Photo by William A. Haviland.

She wheeled, her pleasant face flushed with the heat from the woodstove. "Lord bless us, Ambrose, you did give me a start! What brings you here this early in the day? Has Lizzie took ill?"

"Lizzie's right smart, I cal'late." He could still feel her grasp on his nostrils.

Charlene smiled. "Didn't know but what she was took with somethin' at the Grange last night—both you leavin' so sudden like." Was there a hint of mockery in her voice. "Didn't even wait for a slice of my custard pie."

"No, don't reckon."

"And we was all havin' such a lovely time, too! Ambrose, you dance just as light as when you was a boy."

Happiness always made him tongue-tied. He cursed himself now, then remembered his gift. He proffered the sodden newspaper; "Don't cal'late ye get much fish now Gooden's gone," he said.

Her eyes clouded for a moment; then she accepted his offering: "For me? Oh Ambrose, you was always the most thoughtful boy I knew!" Her eyes showered him with the old affection. "Now you just set in the patent rocker by the cookstove, while I put this down cellar. And keep your eyes on my preserves, do, while I tidy myself up a bit. Don't often have callers this early in the forenoon."

Left alone, Ambrose appraised the shining kitchen, so much the embodiment of its mistress. None of that slightly sour smell characteristic of so many of the butteries on the island, including his own. His eyes roamed from the shiny stove to the enamel sink and the full tumbler under the pump. The day was warm, even at this hour, and the mile of road had been dusty. He raised the tall glass and tossed off the clear, cool liquid at a gulp.

"Why Ambrose!" Charlene cried from the doorway, "whatever are you doin' of, drinking the waterglass I was going to put down my eggs in!" As she came over to him, laughter and concern struggled for her features. The awful, gummy aftertaste struck him, and he gagged. Suddenly she was all compassion. "Oh, you poor poor boy!" For a moment she held his head against her comfortable bosom.

Ambrose choked. "Charlene," he said, "I don't know as it says anything about coveting your neighbor's widow, but the Good Book tells us the wages of sin is death. I've been goin' agin God's ordinances." He fled into the morning sunlight.

As he hastened back to Lizzie, he could picture what was happening to his interior. He passed Hector Haskell, on the way to the fish factory.

Fig. XI-5. The store of "Jean Baptiste" (in real life, Arthur Mussells).

"Hector, I'm not long for this world."

"That so?" Hector was never one to talk much; he'd hardly hesitated in his stride. But anyway, he wouldn't understand how Ambrose's stomach would gum up, the valves of its entrance and exit close once and for all, his intestines choke up solid, like they was packed with concrete—

As he came abreast of the small brown store, he caught sight of Baptiste opening a can of paint on his stoop. Ambrose never could understand why a Bluenose from Montreal and a druggist by profession should have come to set up business here. But Robert seemed uncommon happy chugging about the islands weekends in his little one-lunger, peddling "Nature's Remedy"— Well, at least a druggist would have brains to see what waterglass could do to a body.

"Oh Robert," Ambrose groaned sepulchrally.

Baptiste laid his hammer by and raised his eyes. "You look like you was goin' to a funeral."

"By King, yes Robert—my own! That careless woman—"

"Careless woman"?

"Robert, I'm not long for this world!"

"That we leave to le bon Dieu, my friend." Baptiste meditated the quid of dulse he had learned to chew in the provinces. "You look healthy enough to me."

"Healthy! Appearances can be deceiving, Robert. I've just drunk a whole tumbler of waterglass. My innards will be preserved like a dozen eggs. I can feel it beginnin' to take holt. It's God's judgment, Robert— Well, I must get along home to Lizzie and make my peace while I can—

No, I'm not long for this world. A druggist should know all about this, Robert."

The storekeeper spat a rich brown stream of dulse noncommittally, and turned back to his box. "Ambrose, if you're not quite ready to go yet, I'd suggest a stiff dose of Epsom salts."

"You mean?—"

"I mean, I wouldn't exactly choose the potion, my friend, but there's nothing fatal in a glass of sodium silicate. You and Lizzie should have a long and happy life together."

A long and happy life!— Ambrose trudged down the road toward home—and Lizzie.

XII

Rockland's Ring-Tailed Fourth

Fig. XII-1. The steamer *J. T. Morse* headed out from the Eastern Steamship wharf in Stonington.

This story came to Tom from Leroy E. "Dick" Haskell—the "Everett" in the version here. Dick's identical twin, Elroy "Dunk," is the "Emery" in the story. Elroy was born first, and Leroy was thought to be the afterbirth and was duly thrown into the slop pail by the midwife. He promptly started to howl, and the good lady bailed him out and cleaned him up! The twins looked so much alike that the townsfolk called them the "Two Dickies" to avoid embarrassing themselves in greeting them, should there only be one "Dick" at any given time.

Since the *North Haven* did not come into service until 1931, the steamboat that transported the two boys was an earlier one, perhaps the *J. T. Morse* (see "Leave by the Lower Deck, Forward"). This story was published in *Yankee* magazine in July 1964 (Vol. 28, No. 7, pp 62–63 and 85–87). It is reproduced here without *Yankee*'s editorial changes, the way Tom wanted it.

○ Rockland's Ring-Tailed Fourth ○

Everett settled back in the patent rocker, his china-blue eyes sparkling beneath the frosty fringes of his brows, his words twinkling as he spoke. "The clams in Webb's Cove that year were three tiers deep and each one a monster. But when you figure they brought twenty-five cents a bushel, shucked out, a boy just turned fourteen had to be a pretty smart hand with a hoe and roller to put away twenty dollars. So I guess you know, old son, that when I walk down the slip onto the *North Haven* with Emery—you never see Emery, did you? identical twins we was—I'm feelin' almighty happy with the big bill stowed away in my pants pocket, along with my new dollar Ingersoll, the first watch I ever owned. I'm some proud of that timepiece; before we've cleared the end of Crotch Island, I must have pulled her out of my pocket half a dozen times.

"It's all unfamiliar scenery from there on, and I'm kept busy checking on the islands and the buoys, but almost before I know it we've nosed into Fox Island Thorofare, made a landin' at North Haven, and are movin' out of the lee, past the Sugar Loaves and the Fiddler. The sun's warm, and the Western Bay's all aflutter with whitecaps. The water tower of the Samoset Hotel and the low line of Rockland Breakwater with four gray destroyers lying

Fig. XII-2. The Fiddler. Photo by William A. Haviland.

anchored inside looms ahead like the Promised Land. Not many island boys got to the city in those days, you.

"Once we're tied up at Tilson's Wharf, it doesn't take my brother and me long to hightail it up over the cobbles of Sea Breeze Avenue to the Thorndike Hotel. Its red brick front is all festooned with red-white-and-blue bunting. The stores up and down the street have flags out and windows decorated. Even the poles that hold the trolley wires have little bunches of flags reaching out over the crowds schooling on the sidewalks like fish making for the pocket of a weir. And across from us is the biggest fireworks store ever seen before or since. The buildin's only a story or two high, but to my boy eyes it looked more than a block long—and maybe 'twas. The pavement outside is lined with baskets and bins of firecrackers; the inside turns out to be full of night works—pinwheels, Vesuvius-fountains, colored-fire, rockets. 'By Godfrey Damon!' Emery says, 'ain't it all some handsome!'

"Emery, he lays in a supply at the fireworks store, but I finger my twenty-dollar bill and hold back. If I'm goin' into the clammin' business for real, I'll need a new hoe (the tines in the old man's are wore halfway down just grubbin' in the rocks and muscle ridges), and I'll have to buy me a new pair of hip-boots. Marm's birthday is only four days off, too, and she's been makin' do all too long with a battered old coffee pot with the handle broke off.

"When the parade the folks are waitin' on the curb for comes along, we can't get excited about it for the most part. Over to the island, all we've got to lead off is the Stonington High School Band, and here they must have half a dozen in line; but except in size this don't differ much from our usual pattern—the Masons and Odd Fellows with their banners, the decorated Model Ts, the floats, including the tableau by the Grange decorated with evergreens and them hatchet-faced females, fat and thin, old and not quite old, all decked out in yards of gauze as angels and Pomona and peace things. But the two companies of gobs that swing along at the end in dress whites, with their big, brass band and drums and corps is quite another matter. We boys trail after them till the parade breaks up.

"B'um'by we board a lumbering old trolley—first trolley car we ever seen—on the Camden and Thomaston Street Railway, bound for Oakland Park. Things at the park is all good enough, what with the ball game and the races for boys under twelve and girls over sixteen (you know how these things are run) and the greased pole with a ten-pound ham at the top for reward. They've got an old alligator in the pool there, and when he surfaces Emery hits him right in the eyes with a stream of tobacco juice. That critter dives some fast!

"We take an open trolley back in time for the fireworks, a settin' in the little seat right aft of the motorman. 'Open 'er up, Cap'n,' Emery says. And he does. And we sit there as she pounds down the rails along the foot of the Camden Hills, with the wind blowin' our hair fer ways from Sunday. 'Whooee!' Emery says, 'this is what I call travellin'!'

"Back in town the crowd has growed, and the Navy's pretty much took over. You bring in just about every able-bodied soul from a radius of nigh onto thirty miles and add to that fourteen hundred gobs set on makin' the most of shore leave, and you've got a mob that pulls the poles of the clangin' trolleys off the wires and that kisses half the girls that pass.

"There seems to be a regular pattern to the crowd—up one sidewalk to the Rankin Block at the north end, with its old cannon and pyramids of iron balls and its tablet in memory of the veterans of the Civil War; then down the other side of the street to a little short of where the trolleys turn west to Thomaston. And firecrackers in the air everywhere without letup, with dynamite torpedoes and cherry bombs goin' off under your feet.

"Emery tugs at my sleeve towards the long string of electric bulbs in front of the fireworks store. 'It's your money, Emery. You go right ahead if you're a mind to.' I say, 'But I got to have that clammin' gear down to Cree's Hardware. I ain't broke that twenty yet, and I don't aim to now.'

"It's getting' along toward nine-thirty in the evening, as I mind, when we spot this big gob and his buddies out in the middle of the street in front of the Thorndike. We've seen him in the crowd that's filin' down celler earlier in the evenin'. We boys wouldn't know why, but Maine's had lots of practice being a prohibition state. A trolley's just rattled up the moderate grade toward Camden, and the big fellow's busy layin' this monstrous rocket into the groove in the rail provided for the flanges of the car wheels. A piece of punk is smolderin' in a pal's hand. Part of the crowd has stopped to watch. The gob leans over to sight lovingly, like he's a member of a gun crew—which perhaps he is."

Everett leaned back in his rocker, hands clasped over his ample paunch, eyes contracted small as berries by the grin that had possession of his ruddy face with its mobile laugh lines.

"Lord deliver us!" I said. "Do you mean to say those gobs actually?—"

Everett looked dour for a moment. "Old son, when I'm rememberin' I don't relish bein' interrupted," he said.

"Well like I say, this big sailor sights once again, then roars: 'Fire!' His pal puts the punk to the rocket's stern, and off she goes up the street, past Perry's Market a howlin'. She leaves a trail of smoke in her wake, while the sailor jumps up and down like he's lost his senses. Then up to the no'thard there's a terrific wallop that rattles the windows, and these beautiful red and green balls of fire fly out into the street in all directions.

"The next one's launched with a tremendous swish, slowly rises up from the rails till she's abeam of O. B. Gonia's shoe block at the height of maybe ten or twelve feet. There's a bang again, and then she lets go with a shower of gold.

"We've been noticin' there's a mess of sailors schooling around the old cannon—and of course a lot of girls from town. Among other advantages to romance, it's not too brightly lighted up there; in fact, Rockland's just changin' over from the old gas lamps. The boys ain't too occupied but what they can see the fun in the new game. 'Course, they're at a disadvantage, deah—being as the track runs downhill from them, and they're further from the source of supply. But they dig holes in the turf near the cannon, get a supply of rockets and aim south.

"That crazy brother of mine's standing halfway out in the street now, unmindful, fairly dancin', 'Holy sailor!' he shouts, 'Holy sailor!' I yanks him into the doorway. 'You gosh darn jackass, you.' I tell him. 'With all them crackers you still got stuffed in your shirt front, if a spark was

Fig. XII-3. Steamer *Vinal Haven* sometimes made the run from Swan's Island to Rockland. Here she is off the slip at Stonington.

to get to you, you'd go up like a powder magazine!' Before long them rockets was flying back and forth at a great rate.

"Most of the stores have closed by now, except those that sell refreshments, and the fireworks store. Folks have crowded back against the shop fronts and into doorways. There's cheerin' and challenging. The boys in uniform are really whoopin' 'er up.

"Then from the head of the street, comes a deep-throated roar that shakes the pavement under our feet. Don't ask me how they done it, but darned if those gobs haven't got a holt of some black powder, poured it into the muzzle of that cannon, wadded her, and rammed the charge home. Well, sir, she belches fire and smoke for as much as five hundred feet; first time she's spoke since Grant took Richmond, I cal'late.

"The big gob down on our end readies his last rocket. The boys are hoarse from hollerin' and grimy as cannoneers. Havin' been down cellar a few more times, they're a mite slaphappy, so before their chief can really get this one squared away, the gunner's mate sets the match to the fuse. She starts an erratic course up the rail, raises herself a few feet, then veers to port. The crowd gives a great roar. 'Jesus,' Emery gasps, 'the fireworks store!'

"Straight through the windows in the open front she screams. I wish you could have seen them customers and salesgirls pour out of those doors. Before we can shake free of our paralysis, all hell's a-popping inside. Firecrackers go off by the pack, like the rattle of a machine gun. Skyrockets start a-rocketin', Roman candles a-roamin', pinwheels begin wheelin'; then everything seems to go off with a steady roar. When we look back at the launching place, the sailors have already melted into the crowd. The MPs sure get the Navy off the streets fast after that!

"Sirens scream, and the fire engines come poundin' up along with the police. The heat's terrific, deah, and the crowd's evacuated from the sidewalks. For a good hour or more by my Ingersoll, Emery and I watch the firemen and talk with the man keepin' steam up on the old pumper. Emery's pretty down-in-the mouth. 'Godfrey Mighty!' he says over and over, like he can't believe it. 'Godfrey Mighty, all them lovely, gorgeous fireworks!'

"When we finally drift across to the Thorndike, my watch says two-thirty a.m. The street's still noisy; there's not much sleep in Rockland that night. I know there wa'n't none for me, on account of how sometime or other when I'd pulled out that danged dollar watch, I'd bailed out the twenty-dollar bill with it unbeknownst.

Chapter XII

ଔ ଔ

"Well, old son, they's some advantage in everything, you use it right. Even to be an identical twin. When I board the boat for home, with just a Canadian quarter left in my jeans, I stay a ship's length away from Emery. B'um'bye the purser comes along to collect for our tickets. 'Oh yes, sonny, I got yours down stern awhile back,' he says. The moment we pull into Stonington on a low drain tide, Emery's at the gangplank with the rest of the passengers to surrender his ticket. Me, I make it safe over the rail to the pier."

Everett slid easily down the seat of the rocker, his legs sprawled out before him, and fished deep into his trouser pocket for the faithful pouch of tobacco.

"'Course, I had to make do without the new clamming equipment, and Marm used the old coffee pot for a mite longer. But what a ring-tailed old baster of a Fourth of July she were!"

XIII

And Tall Waves Flying

The central character in this story is Robert Baptiste, in reality Arthur Mussells, who we met in "That Careless Woman." He and his wife first came to the island as summer people, renting the John Weed house (later Doris Scott Knowlton's, the second house on the right on Old Ferry Road). He then bought the house across the road (next to the last on the left before Scott's Landing Preserve), originally built by Benjamin Scott, whose widow was its last occupant. Arthur raised its roof and remodeled it extensively. Meanwhile, he established his little store at the top of Haviland's Lane (for a photo see "That Careless Woman"). After his wife died, he raised its roof for a second floor apartment, sold the house by Scott's Landing, and moved into the apartment with his adopted daughter Nina (Zerilla in the story), until his marriage to Amelia Carver.

Amelia Carver is the true identity of the story's "Bernice Hardie." She was the second wife of Fred Carver, who owned Hog Island and its farm. "Wolf's Head" Island is in reality Hog, to which is attached by a sand spit Fiddle Head. In 1891, Fred and Amelia began taking in summer boarders in their big house (which still stands today) and several cottages until Fred's death in 1919. After that, Amelia and her sister lived alone on the island, until Arthur Mussells came into their lives in the 1930s.

Arthur never tired of "chugging around" in his boat. One day in 1938, when he was out on the water, Amelia saw his boat moving in a strange way; he had died of a heart attack.

Chapter XIII

○₃ AND TALL WAVES FLYING ○₃

Robert Baptiste stuffed a liberal supply of dulse into the front of his mouth, placed his pad and his charcoal crayons carefully under the bow deck, along with some pressed meat, a loaf of bread and a jug of water, and hauled in the kedge anchor. Then, while his little open boat, built close to the water and hardly larger than the skiff she towed behind, drifted out with the tide, he got down slowly onto one solid knee, pulled up his shirtsleeves under their pink arm-bands, and primed the carburetor of the three-horse Mianus, last of its era. He flipped the wheel over several times by its brass handle, the igniter points made contact, and he was on his way to the tune of an even, one-lunged bark from the exhaust.

Monday through Saturday, seven a.m. to nine p.m., he tended out on the groceries, the "tonic," the little stack of miscellaneous hardware, the patent medicines and simple remedies with which he'd once been so familiar—and the single glass case of penny candies. Under the counter,

Fig. XIII-1. This photo shows Tom Haviland cranking over the flywheel of his "one lunger" Mianus engine. His boat and engine were not unlike Robert Baptiste's.

he kept a box of five-cent chocolate cream cakes especially for the boy from away; no use to put them out in plain sight, for then he couldn't keep them in stock—they sold out in no time. Neighbors dropped in for a loaf of bread, a package of corn starch, or Arm & Hammer Soda; the heft of their trading they did at the stores down at the village.

Weekdays, the small, brown general store might be his tyrant, but now, as on every fair Sunday, distant islands beckoned. He knew the bay as he knew the palm of his hand; no need for charts. And no island he'd not explored. Right now, Crow and the grassy point of Bradbury were in his favor, for wild strawberries were ripe and in abundance, and as with the raspberries which would come later, the supply was more than ample for the gulls and himself. He liked always to pick beyond the present need, bringing enough home in the bailing can to put up a jar or two toward winter. The picking done, he might get out the clam-hoe and have him a mess, steamed in the old way, raking the embers of a driftwood fire from off the heated rocks and covering clams and rocks with a blanket of rockweed wet from the ledges.

The afternoon was his to spend in a variety of ways. First, perhaps, he might spread out on his back in the long grass under a fir tree and watch the white clouds drifting, or pull his straw hat down over cornflower eyes to rest on his close-clipped mustache, dozing off amid the heady fragrance of juniper and bayberry. If the bay had been flat calm, as usual in the forenoon, it might well blow up, but this was no concern to Robert; he knew that by evening the waves would subside again, and he could putt his leisurely way homeward in the glory of the sunset—reds, pinks, orange, till the sea itself was a painter's palette. Meanwhile, he could brace his back against a granite boulder, take his drawing pad on his knee and sketch some bold point making out on the far side of a cove. The rocks he drew were a mite stiff, he'd be the last one to deny it, and the whitecaps a bit regimented in their march up the shore—after all, he'd had no formal training—but when he got them framed in the gray, worm-riddled molding he made from old pilings, the summer folks seemed eager enough to buy his "primitives."

"A solitary," folks called him—too much off to himself in that peanut shell of a boat. Well, he had found these stolid farm folk or fishermen could not share the sensitive feeling for nature that was his by reason of his French blood. To them, a tree was potential pulp; the sea was a realm to be plundered of its herring, cod and mackerel, or to be fathomed by a lobster pot at the end of a long warp and buoy; and to them the Camden Hills at twilight were less than a bridge to eternity. Marie and he had used to read poetry together sometimes; Longfellow and Whittier and Robert Frost—these saw deep down into nature and into man. But Marie had been gone these three years, just after Zerilla, woman grown, had left for Boston. More like their own daughter than a niece, Zerilla. Why did all the yowuns have to go tootin' off to the city? A body's soul could rot there, away from the hills and the woods and bright water. He'd never regretted selling out his little drugstore, though Montreal was no worse than most cities; from there he'd made his way unerringly to the sea.

As he put the wheel over for Crow Island, giving Half Tide Ledge a wide berth, his thoughts carried him back to the last two years Marie and he had shared together before she was taken. His knowledge of pharmacy had spared her poor arthritic hands and legs some pain, but she could no longer walk with him in the evening down the winding path that led from the back of their store to the limestone bluff and its view of the darkly silhouetted islands with their lights—Eagle, Owl's Head, Goose Rocks—flashing their message across the miles. Confined to her dooryard, she still contrived to look up at the stars and maintain communion with nature they both loved so well. And then the inevitable—

When Zerilla came back, summer before last, she'd livened things up around the store. He felt a glow just remembering. The young people began coming round evenings or stopping by on the way home from the ceremonial of watching the *Pemaquid* dock. In addition to 'Rilly, the core of the nightly gathering was young Max and Emery and George—the homely, quiet one, but full of laughter—the stately Nitelle, some of Amos' breed, and fun-loving Cap'n Wines Eaton, still as much a boy as the rest of them, roaring, playing his practical jokes, loving the world. Robert laughed now in sympathy, it was all so vivid for the moment.

He had rigged up a peg board—simple thing but a real inspiration, a pattern of twenty-penny nails in a wooden base, with iron rings to toss over, about the size you'd see in a merry-go-round at Bangor Fair. Quiet George and Cap'n Wines, with his big cigar, had become acknowledged experts, unerring in their aim, and as such the choosers of sides. The young people became tense, the air electric; the girls played, with little feminine shrieks of pleasure and despair, 'Rilly easily the best of them. "Now then!" Wines would shout, "Get them last two on, George, or you're cooked as a fish chowder." Or George would say in his quiet way, "We can't take that point; Treeshie stepped over the line when she tossed." The onlookers became violently partisan, cheering their favorites on. Losers treated to Moxie or birch beer. He called to mind certain nights when, all too soon, it was time to draw the solid shutters and peg

Fig. XIII-2. The *Ella Pierce Thurlow*.

in the iron bars, with the last of the crowd scattering under the bright stars—a snatch of song here, a few bars of "Merchant's Island" from a harmonica dying away farther up the road. And often 'Rilly strolled off with Wines in the moonlight; smart looking couple, they made—

Then Cap'n Wines put off to sea again, and Zerilla was properly melancholy; a body could see the way things would go!—A couple weeks later, news of the big four-master's arrival in Jamaica—a tough voyage with an all black crew that Wines'd had to drive hard in a blow to keep her from foundering. Within two days the telegram followed: "Cap'n Eaton's body found floating in harbor. Mark of heavy blow on head. Investigation American Embassy under way."

The weekend letter for Zerilla from Wines with details of the stormy voyage was truly a voice from the grave; "The good ship *Ella Pierce Thurlow* lies safe in port. God be praised. For a time, there, it was touch-and-go whether we'd make it. Now there's not a breeze to break the tropic heat. I've taken to sleeping on deck. Wish I was with you tonight tossing them rings . . ." Big, blustering, warm-hearted Cap'n Wines! 'Rilly packed for Boston and no one, seemed like, had the heart for the peg board now—or could be they were just tired of it.

Robert pulled himself out of his reminiscences forcibly. The air was bland, the ripples were all a'sparkle. Off in the channel by Hard Head, a school of porpoises were playing; the air was white with gulls swooping for the herring a lobsterman dumped from his spent bait pockets;

overhead two terns zigzagged their erratic course with shrill cries. And could it be that he caught the fragrance of wild strawberries this distance from the little deepwater cove in which he usually landed?

Very much in the present again, he looked with pleasure at the approaching sand-beach; a few moments later he had anchored and cleared away the dinghy for going ashore.

It was at the time that raspberries were ripe on Butter Island—his "Raspberry Sunday," he called it, with a twinkle in those wide green eyes—that Robert noticed the little open launch lying to the east'ard. He had made his way slowly up the island's central rocky hill from the dense bushes on the southeastern point, always lush because of the guano around their roots. He trod with care, to avoid the gray nestlings which hid there or an occasional setting of late eggs, picking berries as he went. The parent gulls swooped and dived overhead with anguished cries. Coming to rest on the rocky cairn some previous climbers had piled on the summit—summer folks he guessed; they were always doing senseless things like that—he swept the horizon with his eyes and folded all that he saw close to his heart. He had heard tell, from some of the island seamen, of the blue Mediterranean; surely it could be no more deeply azure than this, its bosom dotted with darkly wooded islands, the blue-black Camden Hills bounding his world to the west, the notched summit of Isle au Haut rising to the south, much as his fellow

Fig. XIII-3. The farm on "Wolf Head" (in reality, Hog Island) ca. 1930. Past the barn is the "big mansard house."

Frenchman Champlain must have viewed it long ago. When his glance fell to the foreground, he noticed the small boat had not moved. There were women-folk aboard; even now one of them, having spotted him against the almost cloudless sky, was waving something white. In trouble, they were. Well, he had pretty much his quota of rasps; he started down to the cove where he had beached his skiff, with that loose, easy stride of his, lean body thrust slightly forward from the waist, stiff straw on the back of his head. He had no reason to rush; the boat was likely to be there for some time.

When, some fifteen minutes later, he brought his little craft alongside, the taller of the two spoke: "I'm Bernice Hardie, from over on Wolf Head, and this is my sister. Our cussed old teakettle has given out on us."

"Ayuh," he said . . . Fine figure of a woman, her dark hair windblown over the gray-green eyes and the tanned face. Must be forty-eight-ish, he judged. More annoyed than concerned at her plight, she struck him as quite capable of handling most problems for herself.

He'd heard of the Widow Hardie. Since her husband's death three years ago, she and her sister had continued to live in the big mansard house on their island. In the wintertime, when the bay sometimes iced clean out to Cape Rosier, there were spells the two had no contact with the outside world, but Wolf Head was nearly self-sustaining and the cellar was well stocked. Folks said that though she read too many books and was a mite queer that way, she could do a man's work.

Robert climbed aboard and looked things over. "It's your ignition, I cal'late, but she's jump-spark, and all I ever been acquainted with is make-and-brake. I'm afeared I can't help you any."

"Then perhaps you could tow us home?" Her deep-set eyes were persuasive.

"This craft hasn't got much power, but we've got all afternoon. I'm willin'. Now we'll make my tender fast to your stern cleat. If you'll just pass me a line and feed it through your bow chock—"

Fortunately, the usual afternoon breeze had not come up; with the wind setting in against the tide downriver, this could be a pretty choppy spot. Now and then during the hour or so it took his little boat to snake the Widow's boat to its mooring in the lee of Wolf Head, he looked astern. The ladies seemed completely relaxed; each time the Widow waved vigorously. He didn't know the island as well as most others; with people living there, a man hesitated to intrude.

He couldn't well refuse the invitation to supper and to explore a bit. The island rose high from the beautiful half moon of beach with its pier

Fig. XIII-4. The pier and boat house on "Wolf Head," about 1930.

set on solid cribs and its boathouse. His eyes roved over the house on the crest of the rise, over the ample barn with its yards and enclosures and on to the heavy stand of spruce in the background. No rocks or bushes intruded into the fields which sloped gently off to the north, ending in a deep deposit of clamshells at their seaward end. He pictured the generations of Penobscots who had come downriver summers to camp and fish, leaving flints and arrowheads behind them. In the middle distance, sheep were busy cleaning up junipers, bayberry, and small trees. "Sister cards and weaves the wool during the winter months," the Widow Hardie said. "She's right smart at it."

The hay stood ripe for the mowing. "Bernice and I get it down with hand scythes," the stout sister said. We made us a little two-wheel hay cart. We'd thought to hitch one of the cows to it, but we couldn't break her to harness, and anyhow, it don't seem hardly right to make a cow work double for her keep, so we tug it in ourselves."

"What's wrong with me taking tomorrow off," he said. I'll be back home by evenin', 'fore folks begin frettin' about a search party. I used to be a good hand with a scythe."

"You could stay in the camp down by the pier," the sister said. The cot's always made up with a couple of blankets. I'm sure we'd both take your offer mighty kindly."

Supper was a joy to a widower's stomach; a big haddock, wax beans, and beet greens from the garden—and a deep rhubarb pie. "By King!

Widow Hardie," Robert said, "I haven't set a tooth in such crust since my Marie died. A solitary man don't find much pleasure cookin' for hisself."

After dishes were washed, the three of them stood on the corner of the piazza. Breathtakingly beautiful, the liquid notes of a hermit thrush came to them from a nearby clearing. *Is there anything so truly lovely?* he mused. The lights in the little cottages at the cape came twinkling on, one by one; the beacons off Western Island and on Pumpkin took up their incessant blinking, and up toward the river's mouth the red and green running lights of a pulp barge shone like jewels. The watchers were long silent, greedily drinking it all in. Then the Widow Hardie's voice came to him softly.

> Upon these underlands the vast
> And ever-climbing shadows grow.
>
> And strange at Ecbatan the trees
> Take leaf by leaf the evening strange.
> The flooding dark about their knees,
> The mountains over Persia change . . .

Robert's Gallic heart warmed, though the lines were strange to him; he had not thought to hear poetry in these parts.

She mistook his start of surprise. "When I was young," she said, "father—he taught at the U of M, you know—used to read to me. He'd give me candy, ribbons, and suchlike as rewards for memorizing poetry. I guess I've never stopped. When we're iced in, winters, I read aloud while sister cards the wool."

All too soon, it was time for Robert to retire to the cabin.

Haying was Monday's sole concern, as promised. His smooth scythe whispered to the ground; stride followed stride ahead; the perspiration started; he could feel the muscles of his back and shoulders loosen. Yes, he was still a good hand in a hay field. For lunch, the Widow Hardie's oven produced a shortcake, toward which Robert's pail contributed a quart or so of red-ripe, sun-warmed raspberries. The afternoon in the fields was a repetition of the morning; he had really hit his stride now, and took pleasure in it.

That evening, when he dropped the mud-hook in home waters and rowed ashore, he had to own to a physical contentment he hadn't known for the past two years.

Chapter XIII

෴ ෴

In the time of blueberries and gooseberries, he allowed he'd have him a good week's vacation; he'd found the cabin on Wolf's Head comfortable and the fishing good. He managed to catch him a sizable cod for the Widow's dinner, on the way.

When he dropped anchor in the cove beside the unfamiliar outboard, he had a premonition. The fancy clothes hung up in the camp—slacks, vivid sports shirts—told him he was in for company and perhaps for trouble. Sure enough, the chap was sitting on the piazza with the ladies, watching with the aid of glasses the regatta of one-designers out of Buck's Harbor. Laid over to a favorable breeze, they were like so many little white moths skimming a field of delphinium blue. (He rather liked the figure.) "Robert," the Widow said, "I'll make you acquainted with my late husband's cousin, Joel. He's been with us a week now and plans to stay on a piece."

Without rising, the man took Robert's hand in a clammy grip. "Thought it was about time I checked up on my cousin-in-law; these gals really need a man about the place. What you got in the bag?"

Robert passed it to the Widow; she revealed its contents with a smile

Figs. XIII-5 & 6 (opposite). An outing on "Wolf Head" (Hog Island), about 1930. The man in the straw hat is "Robert Baptiste" (Arthur Mussells).

of pleasure. "Humph," Joel said, "cod! Where I come from we'd as leave eat skunk. This time of year, 'specially, they're full of worms. Now, right after lunch I'll take Bernice over to the main, and we'll pick up a mess of tinker mackerel." Against the Widow's slight gesture of protest, he laid the dank corpse on its bag for the blowflies and yellow jackets. "Now, when I was a boy setting out trawls from a Gloucester dory on the Grand Banks . . ." Robert sat mute, but the ladies seemed enthralled by the tale which followed.

At supper, Joel held his cousin's chair with a flourish, then quickly slipped into the one at her right, which Robert realized with a pang had been his on visits through the past months. "Thought I might give you a hand at picking your blueberries for the canning," Robert suggested. They're just about at their peak; oughtn't to be left on the vines—"

"Did you say 'picking'?" Joel asked in horror. "Why, the only way, if you're going to can, is to rake them. Saves a heap of time, and broken backs into the bargain. Then you just rig up a simple blower and winnow the leaves and trash. I can throw something together easy enough." He leaned over and patted Mrs. Hardie's hand, which lay lightly by her coffee cup. "Left my car over to South Brooksville. Come Wednesday, we'll drive up to Bangor and pick up a couple of rakes and some gear. It's time you had a change of scene anyway. Sorry," he said, "I can't take the rest, but a sports car only holds two." Robert didn't think he looked particularly grieved about it.

Supper at five meant a long evening ahead, with promise of a full moon unobstructed with clouds. "Thought I might take Mrs. Hardie out for a little cruise in the *Shag*," Robert offered. "There's a spot over on

Bradbury where the herons nest. Right now they're hatchin' out. I've been there when every treetop for a quarter mile radius was full of birds. Quite a sight, it is."

"Why that craft of yourn just crawls," Joel said. "You wouldn't get back till midnight. We'll go in mine. I've promised Cousin Bernice a sail, anyway."

"I'm sure I'd enjoy getting out on the water with two such cavaliers," she smiled impartially. She gathered some wraps, and soon they were aboard.

Ornery bastard, Robert observed to himself as Joel gave a long pull at the starter cord. The engine sputtered, then took hold; the little craft raised herself half out of the water and they were flying. *Ornery bastard, up to no good!* The ladies sat comfortably in the stern; Joel occupied the central thwart facing them, steering with an oblique glance over his shoulder. Robert crouched in the bow, taking the spray as they pounded occasionally into a larger wave. He was a mite chilly and, he had to admit, more than a bit concerned. Obviously, the man knew precious little about boats, for all his talk. Crazy flat-bottomed craft with no hold on the water, if she came into a turn with a sea just so— (Why did outboard owners spend half their lives going round in circles?) Joel and the women-folk were occupied with a sprightly conversation of which he could catch the merest fragments: something about how the man got a schooner back on her course off the Georges when the captain was completely lost. Good Lord, couldn't they see the fellow was a fraud? Robert's own isolation was complete. Why, he'd never had a moment with the Widow since he'd come, and he had matters of importance to discuss—

The nights he and Joel spent in the camp together were little more than an armed truce. It was difficult to be civil to him; God how the man gassed! "What Cousin Bernice really ought to do," Joel said, "is sell out here—she could get a pile for it—and go live in a comfortable little rent in Portland or Boston. She's well fixed already, and I could handle her funds, so she'd be comfortable for life. Wolf Head's no place for two lone females, 'specially in the wintertime." So that was the way the land lay! Handsome chap for his years, his hair still yellow, those broad shoulders, and those cold yellowish eyes. Women had fallen for less. And now Joel and the widow were off for Bangor tomorrow. Robert did a heap of thinking—

Joel was a heavy sleeper, which made the plan feasible enough, and the moon didn't set till well after midnight. Robert was certain the man was no mechanic. Reassured by a resonant snore, he roused just on the point of dropping off, pulled a flannel shirt and pants over his pajamas, and slipped down to the tender. As he'd foreseen, the tide was close to flood, so he didn't have to grate the skiff down the shore. He paddled quietly out to where the outboard lay. It was the work of a very few moments to disconnect the bowl from under her carburetor and drain out half her gas. Then he filled the bailing dish with saltwater and poured it into the tank, repeating the process until the level appeared to him about what it had before. The beacon flashed dim in the silver moon-path, and there was a light still burning, a single lamp, in the Widow Hardie's chamber; perhaps even now she was gathering together the clothes for tomorrow's outing.

He made it back to the shore safely and tied the skiff to the spike in a heavy log. The tide had about two feet to come yet and would blot out safely the footsteps in the sand.

☙ ❧

Robert just happened to be tinkering with his own engine when the two rowed out to take off. He felt no embarrassment at being an eavesdropper. By the time Joel had spun the outboard for the tenth time, while the Widow sat temporarily amidships, her legs drawn up, her rangy body decked out in her best blue silk, Joel was sweating heavily. "Maybe," his passenger said, "she's not getting her gas."

For answer he flipped the choke lever and pulled her through twice. A thin stream trickled down over the carburetor. He threaded the starter again and yanked the line with increasing ferocity. "Maybe," the Widow observed solicitously, "it's the ignition."

He spun the engine fiercely three times in quick succession.

"You sure the battery isn't dead?"

"Goddamn it, woman," he said, "I've got trouble enough here without your yammerin'."

"And I've had enough of your foul temper. I'll thank you to put me back ashore."

It was at this point that Robert, very busy pumping the bilge of *Shag* and tidying her up where she lay, cast off and putted up alongside. "Havin' a mite of difficulty?" he observed solicitously. "Can I be of help?"

"You can land me on the beach." The Widow's voice was icy.

"Well now," Robert said, "that seems like a cryin' shame, what with you all rigged out for a voyage. What say you come aboard and we two light out? You did want those blueberry rakes right bad. I can hire a car over to Brooksville to take us up to Bangor."

⋄ ⋄

For a solitary, Robert had to admit that the day in Bangor was prime. They wandered through Sears, down by the post office, and Freese's big department store, buying a few things that caught their fancy. They had lunch at the Penobscot Exchange, then sat in the little park over Kenduskeag Stream, with the great Hannibal Hamlin looking complacently down at them from his pedestal, and watched the townsfolk as they passed. They were on their way back up the hill to Broadway with its lovely patrician homes of another era when Robert suddenly bethought himself, "The blueberry rakes!" he said. "But could be we can pick them up in Bucksport. There's two good hardware stores on the main street."

"Shucks!" the Widow said, "I don't want any rakes; hand picking's good enough for me. What I was hankering for mainly was an outing—and I've had it. We did have a good time tramping through the stores. I won't forget it soon."

Their course back wound with the river, through Bucksport and Orland, past the great basin of wet mud which the Bagaduce would fill when the tide came in again. Enlivened as their drive was by memories of the day, he sensed that neither felt a need for routine comment on the paintless shabbiness of South Penobscot or on the occasional stands of pine or cedar which broke the long wooded stretches of birch and maple and spruce. "Cities," she said once, "can be fun for a day now and then. But Lord forbid I should ever have to live in one."

Robert agreed enthusiastically: "Ayuh," he said. He passed the turn down to the wharf at Buck's Harbor and continued on to the high, barren eminence before the road dips down into Brooksville and its little millrace dotted with spatterdocks and drove out onto the igneous rock.

"Look, the highland cranberries are 'most ripe," he said. All about their car, wherever hollow pockets of earth had gathered in the crannied ledge and pushing their waxy green leaves through the gray lichens, the solitary little berries were putting scarlet on their cheeks. *Only the blackberries to come now*, he thought; *how the days have flown!*

Beyond and below them lay the bay and its islands: Deer Isle, Pickering, Eagle, and the big Whaleback of Great Spruce Head; nearer at hand, neatly arranged in a row, Hog, Pond, Western, and Wolf's Head with the

Widow Hardie's house looming on its grassy slope. For the moment, she seemed to have retired to a spot too remote for him to follow; her voice came softly, as from a great distance, savoring the words:

> To the watchers of the cliff comes the sound of surf
> The water roiling at the rocks, the island pummeled
> By spray whose fingers worry at the stone.
>
> Under the turning dark, the lights move; the ships pass,
> And the trees and meadows bear wind as in a thousand years.
> The sound of surf and tall waves flying
> Endure, troubling the dreams of night and all lost journeys . . .

"Bernice," Robert said, suddenly conscious that he'd used her given name for the first time, "that cousin of yours—"

"Tiresome old windbag, isn't he!"

"Bernice, you *could* use a man on that island—"

She touched his hand lightly in token, and two sensible middle-aged persons, as dusk came on, they turned the car back toward the spot where they had landed in the morning.

XIV

"Come Josephine"

This piece was inspired by two reports in the *Deer Isle Messenger* in November of 1913 and reprinted in *Island Ad-Vantages* (November 14, 1963). Under Stonington news, the first reads as follows:

> The whistle at the merry-go-round is heard evenings & large crowds enjoy this most fascinating & healthful exercise. Mr. Russ will keep it in operation as long as the weather holds good.

Further on in the same column is this:

> The Wednesday Club enjoyed a ride on the Merry-Go-Round Sat. evenings. They not only enjoyed the ride but the music also. Large crowds are enjoying both the rides & the music & it is the most popular entertainment in town this fall.

Presumably, this attraction was set up at the top of Russ' Hill (Bartlett's Hill in the story), where the ball field is today. This was a favorite location for the various carnivals and circuses that periodically came to the island.

From these two bits of information, Tom built a story that is pure fiction. That said, there is a certain plausibility to the pranks.

ಛ "Come Josephine" ಛ

Above the sound of drills at the quarry on Crotch Island and the heavy exhaust of a lobster boat threading the ledges of the outer harbor, came the insistent crazy jingling of the merry-go-round on Bartlett's Hill. Hubert Knowlton cursed from the very bottom of his being.

The infernal thing had arrived the week before in a brilliant red trailer-truck for an indeterminate stay. Its owner had recruited a half-dozen island youths who, under his supervision, laid the circular track in a level field at the side of the road and bolted firmly together the sections of the machine's gilded gingerbread and mirrors; then they mounted its chargers—black and chestnut, piebald and roan—on the platform prepared for their reception. Last of all, in the grassy plot in the center of this whirling halo, they set up the small steam engine which, through a chain and cogs, drove the silly contraption. The owner—a fine figure of a man, Hubert had to admit—sweat beading his forehead and dripping off the ends of his luxuriant black mustache, breathing deeply through a mouth half open to reveal shining white teeth, surveyed the finished job. Hubert, watching the operation, thought sadly of the contrast of his own stocky figure and unruly hair, his nose slightly pugged, his quite unglamorous flannel shirt and dungarees as revealed in a mirrored section standing nearby.

That had been six days ago. Ever since, afternoon and evening, as he cultivated his garden or took his leisure on the small front stoop, the sou'west breeze had brought Hubert the same dozen tunes, endlessly iterated by its little calliope organ, with the wigged figure of a courtier and his lady all dressed in white with gilt trimmings—French, he supposed—who at appropriate intervals, with stiff mechanical movement, clashed a pair of cymbals together. Even now the music intruded itself upon his thoughts:

Come Josephine in my flying machine,
Up she goes, up she goes . . .

He picked up the *Chronicle*, which lay crumpled at his feet and read again:

Our town is delighted with the merry-go-round, which its genial owner, Mr. Green, has set up on Bartlett's Hill. As the horses revolve, the organ regales island music lovers with a variety of popular and classical selections such as it has not been our fortune to hear for some years past. While children find delight in the ride, the ladies of our town seem especially drawn to Mr. Green and his refined source of entertainment. Hardly an hour during its operation but what some of our most attractive and intelligent young women may be seen sitting gracefully in the saddles of his spirited steeds and regaling themselves with the strains of the organ.

Next Friday, on the full moon, the Rockbound Rebekahs plan to attend in a body. Mr. Green is a truly accommodating gentleman, helping the ladies mount to the saddle, reassuring those who might otherwise be made dizzy by the circling of the merry-go-round. It is our hope that he will tarry long among us . . .

It wasn't just the noise and clatter—the shrill whistle of the steam engine each time the contraption prepared to start on another series of gyrations, the clanking of the wheels over the joints in the track, the blaring of that insufferable organ:

Come Josephine in my flying machine
Up . . .

No, for Hubert the affair took on serious overtones: Flossie P. had turned him down two evenings running, when they were in the habit of walking down to the drugstore for a soda together, to wander later out on the steamboat wharf and watch the moon rise over the cleft top of Isle au Haut. And Friday, when the Rebekahs planned to attend in a body, was his regular date with Flossie for the Lady of the Lake at Odd Fellows Hall. Small comfort that several of his friends were in the same boat.

A little too smooth, this merry-go-round chap; beat all how he fluttered female hearts! After he had thrown in the clutch to start her, he stood poised at the edge, let the moving platform gather momentum, then, seeming to pay no attention to the whirling horses to which his back was turned, leaped lightly aboard, his hand clasping one of the brass poles that held up the gaudy canopy. He moved easily from person to person to collect his fares, exchanging a word with his familiars; then, with the carrousel at full speed, leaped nimbly down again. "He's such a *wonderful* person," Flossie P. said. "That simply beautiful smile! And he has such polished manners. You boys could learn a *lot* from him."

"All is, you never get off the island. What with the fairs and carnivals—Bangor, Augusta, Houlton, Portland, Topsham—why, it seems like he's been all over the world . . ." So that was the way the land lay! Well, By Godfrey, he'd never been one to take something like this lying down!

When he enlisted in the sacred bonds of friendship Vergil Weed, tying up his boat after a long Thursday's lobstering, they began to see the outlines of a beautiful plan. "They's just eighteen horses, Vergil. When you haul tomorrow, don't toss them ripe old bait pockets to the gulls; you fetch them up along to my house. While folks are busy with their suppers, we'll ease up alongside that infernal machine; won't be nobody travellin' the roads that time o' day, and we'll go to work. But be sure them pockets is really ripe."

"Don't you worry none, Hubert, " Vergil said. "They'll be so rotten I'll probably heave what's left of my lunch before we get halfway there."

"And some balin' wire, Vergil."

"Ayuh," Vergil agreed, "some balin' wire."

ଔ ଔ

Vergil was more than as good as his word. Though a lobsterman is used to a fragrant bilge, Hubert had to admit these pockets were prime.

Methodically, the two went to work as prearranged, with a wary eye for possible passersby. "In under the horses' tails, old son," Hubert admonished. "And mind you twist them wires too tight to be slipped off. Now shake a leg; we ain't got too much time to spare." The job finished to their mutual satisfaction, they retired with a couple of hefty sandwiches and a bottle of "tonic" apiece to a nearby clump of alders.

Flossie and the merry-go-round man arrived together (had the cuss to supper, she had!), the other Rebekahs on their heels. Flossie was flounced out in a green ruffled gingham with ribbons, her titian hair in curls. She sniffed delicately, as her escort boosted her gently onto a spirited stallion, and turned her wide, green eyes on him in a lingering gaze. "Seems to me," she said, "the fish factory smells uncommon strong tonight." Solicitously, he helped the other ladies—a rainbow of color—onto their steeds, then stepped to the donkey boiler in the center and opened wide the drafts. Next he turned his attention to the little organ. The French courtier and his mate gave a preliminary crash of their small cymbals; a snare drum rattled somewhere in the midst of the pipes, and the concert was on. Soon he would pull out the throttle, and the carrousel would begin its slow whirl. Despite his preoccupation with the rising steam in the gauge, the tall stranger had reason to confirm Flossie's observation: the fish factory *was* uncommon strong.

Among the Rebekahs, a dainty handkerchief was applied to a daintier nose; they were restive; they gazed questioningly at one another. But they had begun to revolve, slowly picking up momentum. And as the breezes swirled about their steeds, lifting a light skirt prettily, rippling stray locks of hair, a smell as of things long dead enveloped them. The merry-go-round man hopped nonchalantly on in his usual fashion—and as quickly off. That dreadful stench was much nearer at hand than the fish factory. Seemed almost these horses were not wood and plaster after all. But no barn smell was quite like this. It was then that the ladies discovered the bait pockets firmly fixed under the horses' tails. Their black-haired idol threw the engine out of gear and braked her. Several of the Rebekahs showed faces green and nauseated already. Hubert and Vergil watched them jump from the horses with little cries of feminine distress. Noses buried now in handkerchiefs and scarves, they fled the scene precipitately. It would take a thorough scrubbing with chloride of lime to make the merry-go-round habitable again.

He had to own it was unfortunate that at the peak of the excitement, Hubert, in his hiding place, could not hold back a hearty guffaw. The confusion was not sufficient to dull Flossie's ears to the familiar deep tones. When she saw him in the P.O. on the morrow, she found opportunity to express herself. "You—you ruffian! I said you had no manners. To treat a perfect gentleman like Mr. Green to such a trick. I'll never speak to you again."

"Aw, now, Flossie," he placated, "a joke's a joke!"

"I mean it. You are a dreadful, dreadful man!— Why, if I was Mr. Green I don't know what I wouldn't do to you."

"He wouldn't do nothin'. He couldn't resk havin' that curly hair mussed. You listen, Flossie, I bet that man has a girl in every port."

She turned a slender back to him and tripped haughtily away.

It was at this point that Lafayette Black, absent by day in the quarries on Crotch Island, decided the carnival man had lifted his plump and platinum-haired Leah too lingeringly onto a horse, and joined the conspiracy. Strenuous action was called for, they agreed, if this off-islander was not to cast his spell over half the girls in the town. Sunday afternoon would be a popular time on the carrousel, and they laid their plans accordingly. Since the horses would stand quiet while the faithful—

Congregationalists and Latter Days alike—attended church, Saturday night after the last tune was played and the last lights were extinguished, on into the hours of Sunday morning nearest midnight would serve their purpose.

Hubert and Vergil and Lafe went about their work methodically; the reflection of the moon, laying a broad path on the water clean to Isle au Haut, provided sufficient illumination, and the shadows about the horses and organ afforded concealment enough. The project this time was of a far more complex nature; though no houses abutted to the field, communication was in whispers.

"Lafe, them dynamite caps. You found some layin' loose over the quarry?" Hubert asked.

"Ayuh. Three's all I brought; figgered we didn't want to blow the goddamn gadget clean off the rails."

"Well, we'll split 'em up between the three of us; you pass one over to Vergil and one to me. And, mind, we want to wire 'em on the track as far ahead of her wheels as we can. I figger if she gets off to a fast enough start—"

"You just leave it to me, deah," said Lafe. "You think I been runnin' a donkey engine over to Crotch Island for three years, Hubert, and don't know how to cut out the governor? Simplest thing in the world. Now let's get to work on this old ferry boat. You got the stillson? Well, take a bearin' on this rod, now, whilst I give it a turn or two—"

The final operation was more intricate. It raised a bit of a sweat even in the wee hours of a cool Sunday morning. "And mind," Lafe said, turning his huge quarryman's hands to the task, "you take off the lock washers and leave them nuts with only a couple threads to hold 'em."

"Seems like there's considerable resk involved in this part, Lafe," Hubert said. "You sure we ain't overdoin' it a mite, old son?"

"Gawd, yes," Verge's whisper rumbled heavily from the shadows beneath the platform.

"No resk, Hubert, I'll be there to throttle her down before that black-haired bastard knows what's goin' on. I'll brake 'er hard—"

ಐ ಐ

Come Sunday forenoon, the merry-go-round man fired up his boiler early, then started the music—aimed to just give a family time to get home from church and put away a solid meal—and ran through his repertoire. The island folk filtered in slowly, the girls and the fashion-conscious decked out in the latest from Sears' Midsummer Catalogue. The men had discarded suit jackets for the most part in the midday heat, suspenders holding up their Sunday trousers, blue or pink elastic armbands keeping shirt cuffs above the wrists. No cloud interposed a saving shadow; the sun made the whole bay sparkle. Mr. Green had strung little pennants about the outer canopy of his machine in honor of the occasion. The brass-work glistened in the sun's rays.

Hubert and Vergil waited halfway up the hill for Flossie and Leah. Their tentative "Hi!" was completely ignored, as the fair ones swept past without a glance in their direction. If the girls hadn't been so confounded uppity, a word of warning might have been in order. Well, if that was the way they wanted it!—

By the time they'd picked up Lafe and trailed the rest of the town up the hill, there was a lull in the music; the owner had mounted a small box. "Folks," he said, "we'll overlook some misguided soul's idea of humor a couple of evenings ago. Aside from that, my reception in your town has been so generous that I wish to invite all those here present—men, women and children alike—to have their first ride of the afternoon as my guests. Step up, folks, onto the finest little merry-go-round in the State of Maine, bar none. Polite, genteel entertainment, for the young and old, a gentle, relaxing ride to the loveliest tunes, classic or modern, on this unsurpassably beautiful organ."

It was playing the Anvil Chorus now. There was a rush for seats. Though the widow Phoebe announced in no uncertain terms that she hoped she had more sense than to climb aboard that whirlin' contraption, a sentiment which Ignatius, Ambrose, and several others echoed, there was a rush by the young and the young in spirit: Chauncey and Clamhead, Penny and Elroy, Waldo and Charlene. Amos, his big red mustache freshly combed, sat decorously with his portly Ida Margaret in one of the swan boats, which were interspersed between the chargers for the kiddies and the more timorous; even poor, stupid old Reuben grinned foolishly as he stood at a horse's head, gripping the reins in his huge paw. The island's loveliest had managed with Mr. Green's help to preempt a little group of the steeds; Leah, more daring than Flossie, sat sidesaddle on a dappled mount, one of an inner circle which would canter almost to the very top and down again as they revolved with the rest.

There was another interval in the music. "Children, adjust the straps about your waists," Mr. Green called, waited a sufficient time, then threw her into gear. He posed for a brief part of a second, back to his oncoming chargers, which were already moving with unaccustomed speed. He raised a foot in the usual nonchalant manner, and taken unexpectedly in the rear by one of his racing horses, crashed flat on the platform, as all three dynamite caps went off in unison, seeming to lift her for the moment a full two inches above the rails. Three of the Rebekahs collapsed indecorously to the platform, wild-eyed and bonnets askew, clutching in a death grip the legs of their erstwhile mounts. Poor Reuben gave a shout: "Take to the bushes, the clam-diggers have landed," and crouched behind a horse's flank, training an imaginary machinegun at an unseen enemy.

On the carrousel rushed through the acrid smoke, at what seemed express-train speed to those aboard. The merry-go-round man lay prone, knocked out beneath the horse's hoofs. The youngsters jumped helter-skelter to the soft earth, but more prudent folk, clinging round their horse's neck or to the brass poles, elected to stay aboard as the lesser evil. Flossie, legs tightly clasped under the belly of her pinto, careened sidewise at a crazy angle, while Leah galloped madly up and down, hands locked upon her brass pole, and offering a liberal display of lacy pink under-things and thigh. *Nothing like getting a good look at the merchandise before you bought it*, Vergil thought, moving in from the fringes of the crowd.

Hubert had reached the edge of the whirling platform. Each time Flossie raced past, her green eyes even wider with fear, hair streaming, green gingham disheveled, ribbons flying, she seemed to have slipped farther toward the underside of her mount. Lafe, having miraculously appeared at the side of the steam engine, was tooting her whistle madly in sharp blasts.

"Let go of the horse, Flossie, and I'll catch you," Hubert shouted above the tumult.

"I don't dast to," she wailed, as she came round again, now well down under the horse's belly.

Several mothers who had small children aboard fainted dead away, but the spectators, for the most part, stood petrified.

Slowly, dazedly, the owner of the carrousel raised himself halfway to his feet, at which moment, precisely, the nuts let go, and the merry-go-round—no longer round but straightening out—leaped the track. Flossie tumbled free and found herself, all weak and watery, in Hubert's arms.

The spectators broke ranks. "Godfrey Mighty she's agoin' down the hill!" But now, at last, Lafe braked her hard, and she came to a jolting stop. Those aboard lay mostly in grotesque groups, collapsed on her platform. Ida Margaret had thrown her huge bulk upon Amos, her locked arms about his neck, so that the swan boat showed imminent signs of collapse.

Leah clung screaming at the height of her charger's arrested orbit, her skirts up around her neck, platinum hair loose down her back. "Lafe!" she wailed, "Lafe, you get me out of this!"

Lafe leaped onto the platform below her. God what shanks the girl had! "Leah!" he called up to her, "Will you marry me?"

She was in a pet. "No!"

"Then stay there!"

"Oh Lafe, no—I mean yes; anything to get me out of here."

"What you might call grudging acceptance," Lafe allowed, "but happy homes have been built on less. Hang on, I'll shin up."

After the turmoil, a great quiet descended; the bay still glimmered out toward the still waters of Merchant's Row. Only the busy little French gentleman and lady, powdered wigs undisturbed, clashed their small cymbals to the organ's uninterrupted tune:

Come Josephine in my flying machine
Up she goes, oh up, up, up, she goes!

Flossie wrenched herself from Hubert's grasp to kneel beside the groggy off-islander.

08 08

The bay was golden now, as the sun fell below the Camden Hills; the air was heavy with the fragrance of pasture spruce and fir which bounded the field. The red truck and her trailer were packed tight with the disassembled merry-go-round. Its owner sat glumly in the driver's seat, one knee badly wrenched. Beside him, Flossie dramatically held a compress upon the large goose-egg on his head, while Leah waved a tearful farewell. There was no crowd there now to see them on their way, only the few most nearly concerned. "Damn fool female," Hubert growled. "When the glamour wears off, she'll come crawlin' back— And damn fool me, I'll take her!"

Mr. Green stepped on the starter, accelerated, and slowly headed down the other side of Bartlett's Hill toward the main.

XV

Devilish Micnopolous

This piece, a fictionalized account of the last days of Deer Isle's last ferryman, returns us to the location of the two earlier stories: "Leave by the Lower Deck, Forward" and "Peanut, a Memory." Four generations of Scotts ran the ferry from its inauguration in 1792 until its last run in 1939. Charles Scott, who was born in 1860, was the great-grandson of John Scott, who began the service. Charles went to sea as a young man and soon had his own coasting schooner. He went on to become a yacht captain, and in 1895 and '99 he served on the all-Deer Isle crews aboard the *Defender* and *Columbia*, in defense of the America's Cup, on the last, as quartermaster. In 1899, with his mother's death and his father's increasing age, Charles took over operation of the ferry, which was to occupy him for the rest of his life.

When Charles took over the service, passengers and mail were rowed across the Reach to Sargentville in a fourteen-foot peapod propelled by two sets of oars (the second set was manned by Capt. Charles Gray). This changed around 1910, with construction of a decked-over scow, towed by an open boat with a "make-and-brake" gasoline engine. Two cars would fit on the scow; later replacements would take up to six. But it was not enough: no matter how large the scows, they could not accommodate the increasing volume of traffic. Nor could they navigate the Reach in hard blows or winter ice. Even in good weather, there was no service after nine o'clock at night until the next morning.

Charles nominally retired in 1934, the year his wife died (she was Lizzie Marshall, from Deer Isle's Marshall District), leaving his son

Maynard to run the ferry its last few years. Twelve days after the ferry's last run, Charles Scott died.

When Tom wrote this piece, he used fictional names, as in his other stories. However, it was so clear who the characters were and what the situation was, that there seemed no point in disguising identities. As for "the boy," that was Tom Haviland himself. Although he was in his 40s at the time these events took place, with a family of his own, he still thought of his friendship with Charlie Scott in terms of the bond that originated in his childhood with a man he regarded as some sort of hero.

Tom took some other liberties in this story as well. Charles' father, William Pitt Scott, did not die at the oars of his peapod. Rather, his last years were marred by increasing dementia, and he died in 1909. Nor did cadets from Maine Maritime Academy participate in the bridge dedication; the academy had not yet been founded.

The incident where Charles and his companion spent the night iced in at the narrows, however, is quite true. So was the use of the expression "devilish micnopolous." And so was Charles' partiality to horses. His last horse, named Blunderbuss, was the last one to carry mail on Deer Isle. Acquired in 1917, she was used for this in the winter months, even after automobiles were in general use. The horse died a year before her owner did.

Fig. XV-1. The Deer Isle Ferry, in the 1930s. Postcard in the collection of Thomas P. Haviland.

A model of one of the ferry scows can be seen at the Deer Isle-Stonington Historical Society, as can one of the actual sweep oars used to steer the scow.

ଔ Devilish Micnopolous ଔ

With the coming of the sunny days in May, Charlie Scott moved a yachting chair, gray with mildew, out onto the gravel walk leading from the kitchen to the road. Later, the luxuriant lilac bush and the horse chestnut would provide welcome shade, but now the sun was benign. Here, at the corner of his trim, white house with its broad veranda, he was determined to establish his vigil. Just within his vision to the right, his ferries plodded steadily to and fro, two scows large enough to hold a half-dozen cars, each towed by a lobster boat heavy in the stern with granite ballast, its power souped up. The boy, who loved the man next to idolatry, found him there with his thoughts.

The ferry had been pretty much Charlie's life. From the time he could first remember, his father had rowed the mile across to the mainland in a peapod, fair weather and foul, putting his passengers on the beach in the lee of the coal wharf. And Charles, as young bloods will, had set out to see the watery world to the west'ard—on schooners, as a hand on Mr. Biddle's great white bird out of Northeast Harbor, as a quartermaster on the Cup racers *Defender* and *Columbia*. It had seemed to him, on his occasional visits home, that the years took no toll from his dad; the old captain would row his route forever.

Now, as Charles viewed in the center of his field of vision, the ominous gathering of bridge-building equipment on the recently bulldozed point just behind Stave Island, his mind carried him back— The bad news had reached him when the yacht put into Bermuda. Winter was well past, and the ice that always made ferrying hazardous had been sometime out of the Reach. Folks had sighted the peapod floating bottom up over by Byard's Point. The day was not unusual—a southwesterly that raised a slight chop in the Narrows. The doctor said 'twas probably his heart had taken him.

So Charles had come home to marry Lizzie and take over the ferry—carrying his occasional passenger, transporting the daily half-dozen sacks of mail. Come winter time, he had Charlie Gray as his father had, to give him a hand with the mail, dragging it down from Sargentville post office

Fig. XV-2. Winter at the ferry landing.

on a rickety cape racer, bucking the ice in the Reach, then harnessing up the chestnut to the one-seater for the five-mile tug through the snow to Deer Isle village. Gawdfrey Mighty! It was rugged sometimes, when the salt ice was tender, and they'd face the zero blasts, pushing the small boat ahead of them on the frozen surface; particularly when she broke through unexpectedly, and they clambered over the gun'ls, woolen socks and boots freezing cold from the dunking. He could still mind clear enough, over the many years that had passed, the night they'd been iced in at the Narrows in a howlin' blizzard, and he'd kept Charlie Gray from freezin' by poundin' his wet legs and then by slittin' the mail sacks and wrappin' him in the Bangor and Portland papers he found inside— Yes, the ferry had been his life, and his eighty-year-old eyes, their intense blue flecked with brown, looked now with strange disbelief, past the boy, at the collection of bulldozers, derricks, and steel girders assembled across Sally Cove.

He and the boy understood each other, even though the lad was from away. To both, a bridge seemed a thing unnecessary, an anachronism in the familiar scene. Small need to talk; sometimes they sat an hour or more this way—the boy sprawled on the sweet-smelling turf, the gray-haired, ruddy Charles busied with his inner self. B'Gawd, hadn't he, Charlie, been on his toes to keep abreast of people's needs? He'd bought the little double-ender with the five-horse Mianus when his Bessie, for whom she was named, was only a babe in arms? The first powerboat in the Reach, she was, and he'd found Sammy Knight the cripple boy to run her—Sammy, whose mother had dropped him when he was very small, so that he hobbled the road on a single crutch. Agile as a monkey, he was, in a boat, and managed pretty well, crutch and all, on a catwalk or a ladder. Charles knew some folks said he took advantage of this steady chap, so dependable except for the two or three weeks he dropped out of sight in Bangor come fall. Well, King-darn-it! If it hadn't been for him and Lizzie, what could life have held here for a man with a gimpy leg, he'd like to know! In those early days, often they didn't make more than half a dozen trips to Sargentville or to Little Deer with someone who preferred to pay thirty-five cents to waiting for the tide to drop enough for him to follow the cart track 'crost the bar.

Fig. XV-3. The ferry scow and tow boat in the early years.

And though he was a lover of good horseflesh, himself, and never had cared to drive one of the contraptions, when the Model T made its appearance and the roads along the Bay's edge became more passable, he'd got Charlie Gray to give him a hand. He called to mind how curious his neighbors were! The two of them had set to on a pile of good oak planks, got a blacksmith to turn out some ironwork to their specifications, and knocked together a seaworthy little scow that he steered astern of the *Bessie* with a big sweep oar, snaking her in to the gravel beach on a long line, low tide or high. When she first went into commission, though, the trip was more likely to be for Mr. White the telephone man and his buggy—the patient old gray to be unharnessed and led on first, then tied to one of the stanchions of the pipe rail, while they tugged the buggy up a pair of heavy wooden planks. But the cars came in increasing numbers,

Fig. XV-4. The bridge tower goes up. Photo in the collection of Thomas P. Haviland, probably by Cyrus Haskell.

rolling down to the water's edge and so aboard, easing their way gingerly down the planks at the farther shore, then throwing on all the power as they plowed up the loose gravel beach, aided often by the shoulders of several of the audience, with a scattering of sand and pebbles till the road was reached. The rig was primitive but seaworthy, except in a fresh nor'westerly, and he looked back now with pride in his handiwork. So he and Sammy, the scow and the little pinky towboat, all exposed to the elements, journeyed back and forth— And the traffic increased, and he and Lizzie slowly got a few years older, and Maynard and then Doris came. And cattle in the big barn and the powerful big black horse that would tear down the pitch-black, alder-lined road to an occasional political meeting in the village—and a red one that showed them all up on the ice at the Lily pond . . .

ଔ ଔ

As May wore into June and July, Charles' stocky frame found the shade of the lilac grateful. There, by the side of the road, puffing his fragrant cigar and occasionally following the smoke with meditative eyes, while the coffer-dams for the two big towers went in, he talked with friends and cronies. And though he had openly thrown his considerable political weight against the bridge that most islanders wanted, there would always be those who couldn't hold it against him, who recalled his getting the ferry out of her berth in the midnight hours for an emergency. (After a no-good from Stonington had got his own Doris in the hay [pregnant], and the roads to Blue Hill blocked with snow, he'd had to make it all the way by water, praying she wouldn't—and by the grace of God she didn't—die before they reached the hospital. Yes, he knew what it meant to be in trouble!) There were those neighbors in financial difficulties, who had known his generosity freely given, and never a soul was the wiser; and there were the many who, after the ferries carried mainly automobiles, hitched free rides on the scow or towboat to the mainland and back. "B'Gawd," he said to the boy whom he'd helped to manhood over the long summer days crossing and re-crossing the Reach together, "B'Gawd, this ferry business is devilish micnopolous. And what with them new regulations on lights and life-reservers and fire distinguishers, maybe a body should be glad to be out of it all. When Freem Eaton was inspector, in the old days, he'd ring on the four-seven line to say he was comin'. Then I'd drop the boat back out of sight under the steamboat wharf and report everything shipshape when he got there. Now the Coast Guard has got too all-fired curious; they've got to be shown. It's a bad thing when you can't take a man's word! Could be, you, if I was a few years younger we might've worked out somethin' more fittin' the growth of travel, particularly now the Rockland boat's hauled off. Sometimes, B'Gawd, I think my boy Maynard ain't as sharp's he might be about runnin' things." And then, dropping his voice with all the air of an arch conspirator: "They tell me the concrete in them piers ain't settin' worth a Gawd-damn. Made with saltwater, it is, and just like a batter-puddin' inside the shell."

Though early September generally brings a line gale and the nights can be chilly, the days are sharp and gorgeously clear. Charles moved his yachting chair out to where he got full sun again. Still prophesying evil, he somehow could not seem to grasp the inevitability of the thing. To passersby he seemed less alert, bringing himself back from some distant place to answer their passing comments. Between periods spent gazing through the marine glasses that rested on the walk by his side, he dozed a mite; as the steel work for the towers rose and the sides of the roadway slowly reached out from either shore to lock arms over the water, he retired more into the past.

"B'Gawd, Henry Ford will be the ruination of us yet," he said. "Folks want to be friggin' round all day in them motor cars. It's years now since

I had to get me a bigger scow built down to Port Clyde. You take it at Blue Hill Fair week, they'd line up, comin' home time, clean up the hill to the general store. Next thing, nothin' would do but what I'd have to get another large one and keep 'em both goin' steady. Takes it out of a man, it do, handlin' 'em, even with the big powerboats. But that's never hindered folks none tryin' to get aholt of my franchise; 'say there's a heap of money in it, they do. Well, *I* don't know where it is. B'Gawd, after your expenses are paid and your taxes, and . . . It's just lucky I've had good friends up to Augusta to stave the bastards off and to get me state money to plank them runways up the beach and build a breakwater."

Charles was dimly aware that for a taciturn man he was doing a heap of talking; he seemed under some sort of compulsion to get it all out. "And there's more crew to fuss about. My boy's got good men on there, but B'Gawd, ain't nobody you can set stock by same's you used to be able. 'Guess things've never been the same since the year them Gawd-damned rats up to Bangor got aholt of Sammy. Cleaned him out, their fancy women did, and he shot himself! That would have been in 1930. Lizzie never did get over it; he was like a son to both of us."

The staccato of a steam-hammer on steel came to them dimly behind Charles' words. "And the folks travellin' today, they can't be satisfied neither, even with our comin' on duty at 6:30 and not haulin' off till

Fig. XV-5. Charlie Scott in his prime, on the porch of his house—Courtesy Connie Wiberg.

8:30. It's got so's we can't even stop for our noonin', anymore. 'Have to be flyin' about all night, they do, when respectable folks is settin' by the kitchen stove. So now it's one of them suspensory bridges they want, and the taxpayers have got to fork out—all over the state. It'll never support itself, what with this bein' a deadend, let alone pay back on them bonds. You'll see. Mebbe if I hadn't got out of touch with the new crowd up to the Statehouse, I could have got me a modern steam ferry on here; it's all the island needs. But no use perhapsin'. Lizzie's gone three years, come November. A hard worker, she was, and a good wife. I'm not sayin' a word against the children. And Maynard's a good, steady boy, understand, but you've got to have some imagination in this business."

And the boy who had come to say goodbye with another waning season, who had grown up with Maynard and Bessie and Doris, felt a sudden concern for what the next summer would bring. Like some strange sort of parasite, the bridge, as it grew, seemed to feed on Charles' declining strength.

03 03

Letters sent out to the west'ard from the state of Maine over the winter are few; these are not a voluble people:

Fig. XV-6. And shortly before his death. From the obituary in the Deer Isle paper.

"Charlie seems a mite confused sometimes; now he can't set out and watch that blessed old bridge..."

"We're all reasonably well. Weather's so mild they've been able to hang to it steady on the bridge..."

"There's been considerable sickness on the island, but now we're gettin' on to the middle of March we begin to feel we're over the hump for another year..."

"The bridge is scheduled to be opened just before you get here in June.

Fortunately some of father's Republican friends in the Legislature have got Maynard a job as one of the toll collectors, and no more than what's owin' the family after all these years. The bridge will make a great difference in our lives . . ."

"We'll be glad to see you—and summer—again. Though it's still blustery some days, Charlie gets out in his chair on the walk again. But now the painters are just about finished on the superstructure he seems to have lost interest—just don't appear to have much spunk—kind of vague at times. Has spells when he just don't seem to take no mind when you talk directly at him . . ."

Nevertheless the telegram, when it came, was still something of a shock. Good old Charlie! Gone!

The Deer Isle Messenger for the week of June twentieth bore two items of special interest in the midst of the usual gossip of who had visited whom for Sunday dinner, who was off-island, who was speaking next Sunday evening at the Congo church, and the return of some of the early summer folks: The first was an account of the ceremonies dedicating the bridge to traffic. There'd been two bands; the Stonington Lions and Odd Fellows had attended in a body; the color guard and several companies of cadets from the Maine Maritime Academy had marched. Of course, there was a lobster spread for the distinguished guests. The governor had cut a ribbon across the roadway and said that the needs of three thousand island people couldn't rightly be denied—and reminded them that he'd had a big hand in this thing, and he hoped they'd vote Democratic in the fall. The companion piece dealt with the hand of God (strictly nonpartisan), which had removed Charles Scott "whose family operated the ferry to the mainland for over 145 years . . . He was, for the citizens of our island towns, the symbol of an era now happily gone by."

XVI

Uncle Elmer and the Racin' Cow

Given the fame Deer Isle has garnered for its maritime pursuits, it becomes all too easy to overlook the fact that farming was an important component of the island economy for close to two hundred years. This story focuses on that farming tradition. It is based on an actual event. It was published in *Yankee* magazine (July 1963, pp. 66–67, 129–131) in a grammatically "proper" form. Here, it appears as Tom wrote it, which is far more faithful to the original source. That source was Francis Williams (the "Uncle Elmer" of the story), who on top of all the other things he did (shoeing horses, blacksmithing, moving houses, cutting wood—) cut ice each winter in his own and other ponds on the island. The blocks of ice were stored in his ice house, covered in sawdust to prevent melting. In the warm months of the year, he delivered ice to regular customers up and down the island, some of whom (like Tom) refused the lure of electric refrigeration because they so looked forward to Francis's visits.

"Visits" is the key word here. He didn't just deliver ice, he stopped and chatted, trading gossip, commenting on current island events, and telling stories. He was a truly gifted storyteller. These visits might last an hour or more, and he clearly enjoyed them as much as the hosts.

This story is one that he told on one of his visits to Tom Haviland's. When it was published, Francis was so delighted, within a month he wore a copy of the magazine out from passing it around! As usual, Tom changed the names of the "players" in this story, but not the places (though in a few places, he scrambled them a bit). Still, some folks are identifiable: Cyrus Greenlaw was Shirley Stinson; the toll collector was Howard Lowe.

Uncle Elmer and the Racin' Cow

We've just backed the two-ton job up to the door, and Uncle Elmer's inside the house scrapin' the sawdust off the top layer of ice, when I spies the Widow Phoebe crossin' the field under full sail. She picks her way through the mess of boulders and dead automobiles that pretty much cover the immediate territory, heaves to in a little clear space and drops anchor. After she gets her breath a mite, she says to my uncle Skinner—that's for mule-skinner—she says, "I've got a racin' cow in pasture; I know you're figgerin' to serve your route today, and I hate to be a bother, but the critter's uncommon wild. I'd take it kindly if you could see your way—"

Everybody knew Uncle Elmer is the best-natured man on the island. And strong! Stands close to six feet, with shoulders broad as the back of a henhouse. But gentle as a cosset lamb. No job he can't do, and nothin' he won't do for a friend. Already he's tossed the shovel back onto the sawdust, his big broad face lit up with that grin everybody loves, 'spite of the fact he's only two teeth left in front.

"Some o' them Summer Complaints up to Eggemoggin are goin' to run short of ice for their cocktails," Uncle says, "and I already promised Ev to bring back a antique bureau from Mrs. Whitney's auction. But King-darn-it-all, it ain't as if Sam was still with ye. Needs a man to look after these things. Shouldn't take more'n a couple hours out of my day to fix your cow up, anyway."

Uncle Elmer slams the door of the ice house and waves aside her thanks. "Now you just slip back the way you come, Phoebe. Richie and me'll toss a little loose hay aboard the truck and drive her up along to your place. If we warp her stern up to that granite outcroppin' by the pasture bars, I cal'late we can ease Mrs. Bossy aboard from there."

Well, we finds the critter's a mite skittish. She's all for caperin' and climbin'—but not climbin' into no trucks. A racin' cow, like some folks in the same fix, you might say, seems like she ain't got no sense at all. It takes some monstrous tail twistin', and just plain shovin'—like I say, Skinner's strong as an ox—till we get her lashed by the horns to the sides of the truck and a stout halter about her neck. Then Uncle stops to mop the sweat that's runnin' into them sparklin' gray eyes of his'n. "Cussed female," he says. "Under the circumstances, you'd think she'd have sense enough to cooperate. 'Course, you take it fifteen, twenty years ago, you'd just had to walk her to the next farm. But this is the age of progress," he says, "she'd ought to keep up with the times, the old fleabag. Leastways, you'd think she'd understand when a man's set on doin' her a favor."

Figs. XVI-1 (opposite) & 2. "Cut bulls," or oxen, like the ones shown here, were once common on island farms and were used for heavy-duty hauling. By the time of World War II, they had pretty much disappeared from the scene.

As we go lurchin' out Clam City Road, Missouri—Sam names 'er after the old battlewagon he ships on when he's engineer in the Navy—lets out some of the most God-awful wails. "By Godfrey Damon!" Uncle Elmer says, "you'd think we was takin' her on her last ride." He runs a disapproving eye over her bony sides. "Ayuh, she's an ill-favored critter, but under that moth-eaten hide still lingers the spirit of youth and love, as you might say."

'Twan't no more'n ten minutes on the state road, past the Co-op with the lobster boats layin' in their moorin's, to Cyrus Greenlaw's dairy farm, with its big barn and its silo. "You mind Cy sayin'," Uncle says to me, "'Anytime you need my bull, you just go out amongst the cattle in the back pasture. You'll find him there, most likely up by the pond!'"

We couldn't raise a blessed soul in the house. "Well, I allow Missouri'll come out easier'n she come aboard. Supposin'," Uncle Elmer says, "we get 'er ashore. But keep a tight grip on that halter, you, 'cause there's no tellin', if she takes it into her head, which way a racin' cow'll bolt."

"This bull of Cy's, Skinner," I says, "I hear tell he's some spleeny."

My Uncle never has liked to make a show of such things, but almost unconsciously he flexes a muscular upper arm. I mind the tales I've heard, like at the Odd Fellow's Hall, time he was sheriff, when he picks up two beefy lobstermen that's started a scrap, one under each arm, and knocks their heads together till they're ready to call it quits. "I've shod a stallion or two in my time," he says. "Reckon I won't find the bull I can't handle—yet awhile, anyways."

As the three of us rounds the corner of the barn, I see a monstrous beast standin' there; couldn't-a-been much handier. "That bull looks uncommon quiet; you'd think if he was up to his job he'd scented Missouri half-mile down the road."

Uncle takes one look. "Hell," he says, "he ain't goin' to be no good to us. He's been cut. Cy wouldn't leave no bull here. 'In the pasture,' he says."

We can see the cattle moving at the far end of the grass-field, so we lets down the bars and turns Missouri in. Well, she goes prancin' off, and the way she acts with them other cows is a caution. But nary a sign of the bull. "Tell you what," Skinner says, "you stay here to keep sort of an eye on things. I'll see if I can rout out Cy's old woman."

Well, she wa'nt in the kitchen or out with the hens. Finally, Uncle Elmer tracks her down in the rasb'ry patch. "Lawdy, you," she says, "that bull? Cy sold the critter ten days ago, over on the main . . . You tried Waldo Haskell, up Keezar way?"

It takes some doin' to get a halter back on that racin' cow, and some more tuggin' and tail twistin' to get her back into her Pullman Car, but we manage it. As we roll up over the Southeast Hills, where you get a view clean over to Mount Desert, her mooing is sort of plaintive like.

Leastways, we've learned something. When we pull into Waldo's dooryard, we leave the Holstein in the truck and the motor runnin' on account the starter's pooched, and if you can't head her downhill you got to crank her. Waldo ain't to home, but Isabel's hangin' out the wash on what looks like a vessel's yardarm, over to the end of the barn.

She sings out: "Looks like a cow you got there, Skinner."

"Well, it ain't no elephant," Uncle agrees.

"We can't use another cow," she says, stickin' a row of clothespins in her mouth while she hangs a sheet over the line. Then she puts the pins on the line, deliberate like, one by one. "Our bossy's just come in fresh," she says.

"Now Isabel, you don't have to act cautious, like I'm here to make a deal on this critter," Uncle Elmer says. Our passenger offers a mournful note, like Mark Island Light in the fog. "This here's a racin' cow; if y' had half an eye you'd see! We're figgerin' on makin' use of Waldo's bull."

She comes walkin' over then. "Oh, I am tarnation sorry," she says. "I'm sure Waldo'd oblige if he could, but that ornery black critter, what with his pawin' of the ground and snortin' and his tossin' his head and swingin' of his horns was so almighty fierce, Waldo was afeered of what the beast would do when he really had his growth. Made right at Waldo twicet, he did. First time, Waldo had to wrestle him by the horns and throw him; second time, he throwed Waldo. Waldo's sold him across the Reach, over to Carter's Point."

"You know any other bull on the island?" Uncle Elmer says.

"I don't," she says. "Whyn't you take the old gal for a ride over to the Point? You're headed right! Likely she ain't see that part of the world since they hauled the ferry off."

"Well, it's fifteen miles to the Point," Uncle says, "but seein's the critter's so eager, maybe it won't do no harm. "Besides," he says, "I been hearin' some of this stuff about human behavior from my girl Emily, up to Orono, and I wouldn't want to see Missouri frustrated, like they say."

It's getting' on to noon, so he throws the old craft into gear and hauls the throttle way down, and she goes poundin' over the milldam, on up the road past Carman's Rock and over the causeway till finally the bridge heaves in sight. A dollar toll each way and no chance to take it out in

Chapter XVI

Fig. XVI-3. Some "contented cows" on a saltwater farm near the causeway. Note the lead from a fish weir extending out from the shore.

trade up to the stores in Ellsworth or Bangor kinda runs up Missouri's service fee, but there's no turnin' back at this point, I can see.

"Where's your sense of loyalty?" Howard greets us, as he rings up the toll. "Ain't we got bulls on the island can handle this old girl? Kinda reflection on our native sires!"

Uncle Elmer tells him how 'tis.

"Well, they was a bull at the Point awhile back," Howard says. "Ayuh. Cal'late you'll find him there still, if he ain't died of overwork." Missouri gives a long, liquid *moo-o-o*, and we navigate the gravel road to the Point.

"No," says the farmer's wife, "we ain't got a bull no more. The way 'tis, now, folks hereabouts been sellin' their cows to make room in the barn for one of them fancy new cars that look like somethin' about to take off for the moon. Get their milk in a bottle from Tamworth Farm up to Blue Hill, they do."

"By God," Uncle says, "you spose they'd have a bull at that diary in Blue Hill? I'm not easy put off, once I get my mind set on a thing. Besides, I can't disappoint the old girl now."

"Well," she says, "I can't say for sure, but if you go by way of Sedgwick, Bert Gray used to have a big Guernsey bull—showed him up to Blue Hill Fair jist last fall. You can't miss the house, lots of cattle about; white, with a monster big red barn. Folks used to say you could tell who was boss in the family, man or wife, dependin' on the size of the barn. Sets back to the left of the road in a grove of hackmatacks. Won't take you more'n ten minutes out of your way."

"Ten minutes? What's time to a cow," my Uncle Elmer observes. Then, "Thank you, ma'am, I'll give it a try."

Mooo says the racin' cow.

I misdoubt that critter coulda shared with us the view as the road flanks the Reach, lookin' out to Isle au Haut and the islands to the east'ard, the water all asparkle with the afternoon sun and a couple of windjammers out of Camden remindin' of the days when Maine folk was seafarin' folk. Even if we ain't had lunch, and wa'n't likely to, I enjoys it.

Hadn't been off the island for months. But, like I say, I misdoubt Missouri notices; she has what you might call a one-track mind. Females is like that. But when we rolls up to the Punch Bowl Farm, Ole Miss, she lets out another of them Indian-love-calls. This time there comes a heartenin' roar from the rear of the big red barn. Uncle Elmer's never set eyes before on the woman that comes to the house door, nor she on him. But as I say, people naturally take to Skinner.

"Well," she says, "it's plain to see what you've come for. Just you go and help yourself: supermarket, self-service." Her healthy, goodlookin' face is all of a grin. "My husband'll be back b'um'bye."

ଔ ଔ

Sun's gettin' low as the old two-ton job jounces back toward home, screakin' and abangin' and backfirin' on the downgrades—over the bridge, 'cross the causeway, and down the North Deer Isle Road. Our racin' cow's settled down on the hay, and she's a lookin' kinda smug, when Uncle Elmer minds him about that bureau. Mrs. Whitney's lies just t'other side of Carman's Rock. The auction's pretty well broke up, but some summer folks out on the lawn is still hangin' undecided-like around a few battered old pieces of furniture that a body in his right senses wouldn't give house room. Uncle winks at me. "Antiques," he says, pronouncin' the word breathless-like. "Sucker bait!"

"Hi, Mrs. Whitney," Uncle Elmer sings out. "Hope I'm not too late; I brought ye 'nother valuable antique to sell."

"You great ape, you! Don't you go bringin' any cows around here," Mrs. Whitney says. "We coulda used her a week ago to get the grass down around the house, but we ain't got any need of her now. Why don't you just take that bureau along that you're supposed to pick up for Ev, before you get into more trouble?"

Trouble? Sure enough, if there ain't a couple o' them rusticators up from to Eggemoggin in assorted sizes, lookin' like Mutt and Jeff. I've clean forgot till now what Skinner's done to their cocktail hour. Well, we shoves that bureau in beside Missouri fast, but not 'fore the tall one with the ice-cream pants and the floppy hat comes over, lookin' like he'd found a skunk in his outhouse, except of course they're way above outhouses up to Eggemoggin, what with all their fancy plumbin'. "Look here, my man," he says, "what about my ice?"

Uncle throws the truck into gear. "Mebbe life was simpler in the State of Maine when we had prohibition," he says to this feller.

You can't make everybody happy in this world at once, seems like! But, by Gawd, if this fellow from Philadelphy wa'n't satisfied, at least Missouri seemed to be—layin' there beside that bureau as we rolls back home, a-ruminatin' and admirin' herself in the mirror.

XVII

Masters of Fog

To end this collection as it began, we have an essay that, like the one at the beginning, returns us to steamboats and the wharf at North Deer Isle. As with the essay at the beginning, this one is pure nonfiction.

Two of the characters were longtime friends of Tom's: "Gussie" was Gus Webb, stepson of Captain Sam Lowe, who ran a store at the steamboat landing. A bachelor in later life, Gus lived with his half-brother Elmer Lowe and his family in the old Lowe homestead, now the Inn at Ferry Landing, helping out on the farm.

Montie Haskell lived three houses down from Haviland's Lane, having married the aunt of Tom's boyhood friend Chauncey (see "Leave by the Lower Deck, Forward"). Montie went to sea at the age of six with his father, Captain Charles Haskell, later becoming mate. As a captain himself, he commanded several schooners. With the displacement of sail by steam and internal combustion engines for cargo hauling, he signed on with Captain Frank Swift of Camden, who in the 1930s pioneered the summer windjammer cruises. Montie's last command was the *Mercantile*, then one of Swift's vessels.

If the reader is a bit puzzled by references to spars as aids to navigation, these were long wooden buoys, the forerunners of today's cans and nuns. Unlike the latter, they stood high above the water for easy visibility. Colored red and black, rather than red and green, they were replaced by cans and nuns in the 1950s.

Torrey's Castle, too, may be a bit of a puzzle to today's readers. This, too, was an aid to navigation. Built on a ledge off the tip of Torrey's

Island in the Reach, it was a pyramidal affair of iron slats painted red. Such devices were standard day-beacons on the starboard side of a channel; they were replaced in the 1950s with spindles.

Tom received help with this essay from Leroy E. "Dick" Haskell of Stonington, who made sure Tom had the names of people and places right, apart from those he knew.

❧ Masters of Fog ☙

Despite the long years that have elapsed since a boy of eight served his apprenticeship at the oars of a peapod on Penobscot Bay, he has not come to fancy himself man grown, as a thick-weather navigator. When he has blundered into the home mooring or made a rendezvous off Saddleback Island, he has had in all honesty to attribute it more to luck than to skill with compass and parallel rule or to that inborn ability to smell his way characteristic of a Maine-born navigator. And when the

Fig. XVII-1. Steamer *J. T. Morse* on the rocks on the west end of Crotch Island. On July 23, 1924, in a thick fog, she was off course just enough to miss the entrance to Deer Island Thorofare. Courtesy Deer Isle-Stonington Historical Society.

necessity has arisen for the *Cormorant* to navigate Deer Island Thorofare by the needle or to thread the intricacies of the Turnip Yard and the Cow Pen, to the east'ard of Isle au Haut, he has always felt completely happy to turn the helm over to his son-in-law, whose seafaring Haskell ancestors first shaped their course to Deer Isle in the late seventeen hundreds.

The boy's first memory of the bay region is cloaked in fog. Since his father was a railroad man, the lad didn't enter Rockland Harbor by Boston Boat, as all respectable island folk did. He debarked instead at an ungodly hour (memory says four a.m.) from a sleeper at the shabby old Maine Central terminus and was driven through a gray and dripping city to Tillson's Wharf, where the *J. T. Morse* lay softly chafing the piles, waiting for her big sister of the Boston-Bangor Line. She seemed palatial and offered so much to explore that the boy didn't find the wait too long till a steam whistle echoed shrilly through the mist, to be answered hoarsely by the foghorn on the corner of the wharf, and the *City of Bangor*, looming hugely after an exchange of blasts, was berthed at the end of the pier.

The last of the freight was trucked, the mighty one departed on her trip upriver, and then her little sisters slid one by one out behind the curtain of fog, whistles blasting at regular intervals, *J. T. Morse* having first announced her intention by a sonorous tolling of the great bell by the walking-beam on her hurricane deck.

Breakfast in the commodious forward saloon, with its solicitous waiters, was a mere formality, for the boy was eager to make his way up the broad stairway gleaming in its fresh varnish and get on deck. A line from rail to rail kept passengers aft of the needlelike bow, where the forward watch was stationed on such occasions, but the boy could stand below the pilothouse and marvel for the first time at how Captain Winterbotham and his pilot, aloof in the privacy of their high vantage point, made bells and spars unerringly and raised the landing at Dark Harbor in the thinning mist. A bright July sun lifted the fog permanently before she blew for Buck's Harbor—and so she proceeded on a now gorgeous blue day to her terminus on Mount Desert. Many trips were to follow, memorable to the boy, foggy or fair, threading the islands of the western bay and Eggemoggin Reach. When later the *Boothbay* came on from the Blue Hill run, and the *Morse*, in deference to her aging bones, was shifted to the shorter route through Fox Island Thorofare with a stop at Stonington, instead of the northern end of the island, the broad sidewheeler picked her way on her new beat amidst reefs and islands, through the tortuous Deer Island Thorofare, still with the perfect assurance of the blind man who knows every crack in the familiar block or two of sidewalk he taps with his cane each day. Only twice, to the boy's knowledge, did she come to grief (one can hardly count against her the time the *Belfast*, heading into Tillson's wharf, sank her at her berth, or, later, a gentle tunk on Steamboat Rock): one very thick morning when she passed Mark Island close aboard on the starboard hand, she took the next black spar on the wrong side and running out this course struck on Mussel Field Ledge—the Door Ledge, our fishermen call it—on a two-hour ebb tide; and once when Maine Central's steel-hulled *Pemaquid* loomed out of the gray curtain to knife into her bow, forcing her to ground out in Moose Island Cove.

Pilot and captain of the *Pemaquid* were especially cursed by fog, for when other boats were homing to Rockland Harbor in the afternoon, she pushed dauntlessly out to North Haven, Stonington (where she arrived about nightfall), then through the intricate channels off Lazygut, up past Torrey's Castle, and into Brooklin landing. August was the month of fog then, as the man-boy remembers, and with darkness often a heavy pall settled over the water, isolating the little Maine Central steamer so completely that she seemed a sort of phantom ship in a phantom world of her own—nothing else on earth but the beat of her engines, the shrill, regular blast of the locomotive whistle she reserved for these occasions, and the muffled talk of the few left aboard. And in the dark of the wheelhouse, captain and pilot and quartermaster timed the legs of her course, calculated wind and drift, picked up spar and castle with the rays of her searchlight. There were places on that route that called for singular skill in navigation. The boy long remembered making the early morning trip out to Rockland to see the launching of that great beautiful bird, the six-master *Mertie B. Crowley*, on a clear and sunny day—he was about twelve now—and passing through a spot known as the Devil's Den (perhaps old-timers can identify it, though he cannot from his own sailing, nor can he find the name on "Chart 1203." Memory again suggests it was somewhere in the vicinity of the Green Ledges). The tide was at a phenomenally low drain; *Pemaquid* was throttled down to mere steerageway; then the captain signaled "Stop engines," and a long moment later, not before her keel had grated ever so lightly on rock bottom, we were through. One can imagine the difficulty of making such a passage blindfolded by darkness and fog—though perhaps there was a longer way around.

And there were occasional trips when it was much thicker than pea soup, nights so black that the sturdy craft was forced to tie up at

Fig. XVII-2. The steamboat wharf at North Deer Isle, Sargentville across the Reach behind.

Stonington wharf till daylight, and the passengers bunked aboard. It was only eleven miles by road to North Deer Isle landing, and Charlie Scott's little motor ferry ran from there to the mainland terminus—but in the days before the automobile was common on the island, the eleven miles might almost as well have been eleven thousand. One thick-a-dungeon night she did essay it, with the boy among her passengers. When the time was run out, a spar at the foot of the Reach refused to reveal itself. The Boulders, great stark wave-swept chunks of primordial granite, and other formidable threats, lay nearby. The dim probing of her searchlight revealed nothing; after soundings, a small boat was swung from the davits to feel around fruitlessly. Then, on the only occasion the boy ever heard of, the big anchor was dropped, and she lay to at the end of her chain. With dawn, a fault in the curtain of fog revealed the elusive spar not twenty feet off the port bow. But well enough to have been cautious, for just about that same margin of error was later to pile the little *Bodwell* onto the rocks at Swan's Island.

The *Pemaquid* could always count on a reception committee at the North Deer Isle wharf; it was island ritual. Old folk gathered to review the day's events, the young to spark, the very young to spy upon them or play a noisy game of tag among the bags of grain in the long freight shed. One could never tell what wonder might be revealed, as on the

Chapter XVII

Fig. XVII-3. The *Governor Bodwell*.
Courtesy Deer Isle-Stonington Historical Society.

Saturday night Reuben Eaton wove uncertainly up the gangplank, after a day in temperance Rockland, followed by sweating roustabouts pushing a huge *Velie* touring car unloaded upon him in his convivial mood by an unscrupulous salesman. And this still in the horse-and-buggy days! For some years the *Velie* stood poised for flight in the barn door, her brass gleaming, but he never dared drive her out. Yes, even on doubtful nights, when the fog dripped heavily from the trees, a hardy group ventured up the road to see if the *Pemaquid* would make it. Returning from one such occasion with two dozen eggs in a bag, dutifully picked up en route, the boy—and the eggs—found it so thick that in the three attempts necessary to distinguish the entrance to his lane from the stone wall, he lost half his cargo.

And there was the thick night when the doughty craft almost didn't make it—a tense and exciting one indeed! She was past the first black spar on her cross-Reach diagonal from the landing at Sedgwick. Her fog whistle wailed and received no reply; then again, and once again— appealingly, accusingly. No answer came from the dark pier; the agent was not on hand, and his horn was locked in his office. We could pick out the glow of her lights dimly. The men in her pilothouse could gauge their distance from the shore, but no light, no blast to give direction. We heard her bells to cut the engines to low, and we saw her heading directly for Tinker Ledge. We shouted, but no voice, apparently, carried above the sounds aboard. Then Gussie came to life. The wharf was in process of repair, and heavy planks lay piled against the freight house. By now the boy had gained size and muscle; with Gussie to direct and take an end, he lifted a plank high and dropped it upon the flooring with a heavy thud. The others joined them with another plank. Alternately, rhythmically, the heavy three-by-eights rose and fell. We heard a blast of steam from the *Pemaquid's* escape valve by the stack, the hurried jangle of bells for full astern, the mournful wail of the locomotive whistle; then she veered and headed in toward the thud of the planks on the wharf. Now the searchlight's finger picked us out dimly. We caught the heaving line, pulled the hawser through the chock and made her fast.

In later days, when the boy was man-grown and the automobile had sentenced the family barnyard and the "big boats" alike to oblivion, there was still the local Rockland-Swan's Island Line. Year by year the *Governor Bodwell*, a sweet little craft that had survived many vicissitudes, including the ignominy of being given up for a total loss just short of the safety of Old Harbor, devotedly plodded her route. On this latter occasion, the culprit was not fog but pitch darkness and a blinding snow squall in below-zero weather that iced up and silenced the bell on Halibut Rocks. So the Sheriff buoy was made too close to starboard or passed to port; not the faintest ray came to her from Burnt Coat Light, and she piled up on the rocks. But those who said her last rites had failed to take into consideration the ingenuity and resourcefulness of the Snow Shipyard in Rockland. A completely rejuvenated *Bodwell* was to put in seven more fruitful years till she burned one night at her Swan's Island wharf.

Each day, around two, she left the security of Rockland Breakwater behind. If the day were foggy, the horn on the breakwater hailed her as she headed staunchly to the eastward. Casually she eased past the solid granite monument on Fiddler Ledge or more properly the spot where the monument might be supposed to stand, held the Sugar Loaves and the Fox Ears on the beam, picked up the bell by Brown's Head, docked at a moist and dispirited North Haven landing, then navigated the bend of the Thorofare to within range of the bell at Goose Rocks Light. Clear of Widow Island and of the ledges to port, she shaped her invisible course for the entrance to Deer Island Thorofare, methodically ran out her time, counted off the numerous ghostly red and black spar buoys before and beyond Stonington landing, where she halted briefly. Threading her way between Bold Island Ledge and the island itself was tricky business, then setting her course past Shingle Island and its ledge. And so, having made the bell on Halibut Rocks, she passed the Sheriff and the High Sheriff, into Old Harbor and journey's end.

Fig. XVII-4. Montie Haskell, one of the last of the old-time schooner captains. With the decline of shipping under sail, he served for a time on yachts, before signing on with Capt. Frank Swift in the windjammer trade. Photo courtesy Deer Isle-Stonington Historical Society.

And all without ostentation; no gold braid here—at least while Harry Gray was master. A stout, ruddy-faced man, he stood four-square in his little pilothouse raised but a few feet above the main deck and conned his ship, in a plain blue suit, topped by a soft gray felt hat. No matter how seemingly impenetrable the fog, everyone on board knew that *he* knew where he was every minute of the way. (It was under his successor,

Fig. XVII-5. Montie Haskell (left) later in life. His last command was the *Mercantile*, a schooner built in 1916 on Little Deer Isle. Here, he chats with fellow octogenarian Capt. John A. Stephens. Courtesy Penobscot Marine Museum, PPM Image 1D.

Roscoe Kent, that she piled up onto the rocks.) And the boy-man still knew the wonder of it and offered the same homage to the *Bodwell's*—and later the trim little *North Haven's*—navigators that he had on that far-off early morning of his first trip on the broad-beamed old *J. T. Morse*.

☙ ❧

The "little boats" are long gone now. After their departure and before the ready availability of radar, it was left to the lobsterman, unless the weather be unbelievably foul. In a thirty-odd-foot craft powered by a second-hand auto engine—usually without a small boat and often scorning the assurance of an anchor for moments of emergency—he would go into the very boulders and ledges themselves to haul his pots, to perpetuate this uncanny ability to see in a fog-mull. And before the days when the marine engine made plotting a course a comparatively simple thing, he groped through those inevitable days of fog and haze in a sloop, subject to the caprice of wind and tide. He had his big brother, too, guiding the destinies of the Maine-built schooners, with three, four, or six masts, or the little two-masted coasters. A few of these old aristocrats of the sea, like the last of their craft, lingered on into the days of the "Windjammer Cruises" out of Camden. The fog deterred them not at all. Deer Isle's Montie Haskell (veteran of the bowsprit gang on the America's Cup defender *Columbia*), reminisced several years ago, "I tell ye, I used to jump that old craft acrosst the bay out of Camden in a way that made Captain Swift some nervous at times. Couldn't see a thing till we made Great Spruce Head. 'Twan't nothin', really; just like bein' in my parlor at home. I been at it a long time. You! Why, I mind the time when I was mate of father's vessel we made Isle au Haut four days out of Norfolk with a fair wind. Just as we come in by the Western Ear, it shut down thick-a-dungeon fog. Well sir, we strikes up the bay by dead reckenin'. We can hear the whistle on Saddleback to port, gives the Brown Cow a good berth, and picks up the bell off the Porcupines. When we judge we're off Hard Head, we luffs her over and sets our course for Northwest Harbor. I tell you, we didn't see nothin' from the Western Ear till we raised Heart Island dead ahead."

Since Heart Island lies at the mouth of the harbor, that might not be considered too bad a job for, say, close to three hours in a fog-mull. It's an old magic, this navigating blind, that still lingers with some State of Maine mariners, even though their present estate, to some, be humble.

Born in 1927, Carroll M. Haskell (known as "Cabbage" to most islanders) grew up on Deer Isle, graduating from Stonington High School in 1945. Over the years, he did all the things island boys did: besides getting into mischief, he clammed, went lobstering, worked on the granite quarry, went yachting, worked on a lobster carrier running from Nova Scotia to Montauk, Long Island, and served a short stint in the Army. In 1957 he came ashore and married the sister of this book's co-editor (Tom Haviland's oldest child) and took up a career with the telephone company. He is the author of *Growing Up on an Island off the Coast of Maine*, an account of his adventures on and off Deer Isle. Although he currently lives in Philadelphia, he still spends at least four months of each year back on the island.

William A. Haviland studied anthropology at the University of Pennsylvania, where he received his PhD in 1963. He is now professor emeritus at the University of Vermont, where he founded the Department of Anthropology. Previously he taught at Hunter and then Barnard College in New York City. He has done archaeological work in Belize, Guatemala, South Dakota, and Vermont. He studied the bones of kings and commoners at the ancient Maya city of Tikal and carried out ethnographic and ethnohistorical research in Maine and Vermont. His one hundred or so publications include several books, among these five textbooks, one on Vermont Indians (co-authored with Marjorie Power) and three monographs on work done at Tikal, Guatemala. His most recent books are *Canoe Indians of Down East Maine* and *Floating Palaces, America's Queens of the Sea: Maine Island Mariners and the Big Steam Yachts* (co-authored with Barbara L. Britton).

Haviland and his wife, Anita, live on Deer Isle, where he serves on the boards of the Deer Isle-Stonington Historical Society and the Abbe Museum in Bar Harbor.

www.ingramcontent.com/pod-product-compliance
Lightning Source LLC
LaVergne TN
LVHW041335080426
835512LV00006B/467